Praise for *Shearwater*

'This charming and impassioned book meanders, shearwater-like, across a lifetime and a world, a rich tribute to an extraordinary bird drawn through tender memoir and dauntless travel.'

HORATIO CLARE, author of *A Single Swallow*

'This is wonderful: written with light and love. A tonic for these times.'

STEPHEN RUTT, author of *The Seafarers: A Journey Among Birds*

'What I love about Roger Morgan-Grenville's writing is the sheer humanness of it … There are environmental issues and pure natural history in here, but the overall feel of the book is simple, humble wonder. Roger was lucky to have a grandmother who knew how to gently foster a live-wire mind. She loved birds, she loved Roger, and the combination guided him to her way of thinking as he grew older – and this odyssey for shearwaters is the result. Bravo – a truly lovely book.'

MARY COLWELL, author of *Curlew Moon*

'Shearwater is a delightful and informative account of a lifelong passion for seabirds, as the author travels around the globe in pursuit of these enigmatic creatures.'

STEPHEN MOSS, naturalist and author of *The Swallow: A Biography*

'A memoir lit by wry humour and vivid prose … his evocation of the Hebrides is as true as the fresh-caught mackerel fried in oatmeal his grandmother used to cook for him.'

BRIAN JACKMAN, author of *Wild About Britain*

Praise for *Liquid Gold*, by the same author

'A great book. Painstakingly researched, but humorous, sensitive and full of wisdom. I'm on the verge of getting some bees as a consequence of reading the book.'

CHRIS STEWART, author of *Driving Over Lemons*

'A light-hearted account of midlife, a yearning for adventure, the plight of bees, the quest for "liquid gold" and, above all, friendship.'

Sunday Telegraph

'*Liquid Gold* is a book that ignites joy and warmth through a layered and honest appraisal of bee-keeping. Roger Morgan-Grenville deftly brings to the fore the fascinating life of bees but he also presents in touching and amusing anecdotes the mind-bending complexities and frustrations of getting honey from them. But like any well-told story from time immemorial, he weaves throughout a silken thread, a personal narrative that is at once self-effacing, honest and very human. In this book you will not only meet the wonder of bees but the human behind the words.'

MARY COLWELL, author of *Curlew Moon*

'Beekeeping builds from lark to revelation in this carefully observed story of midlife friendship. Filled with humour and surprising insight, *Liquid Gold* is as richly rewarding as its namesake. Highly recommended.'

THOR HANSON, author of *Buzz: The Nature and Necessity of Bees*

'Behind the self-deprecating humour, Morgan-Grenville's child-like passion for beekeeping lights up every page. His bees are a conduit to a connection with nature that lends fresh meaning to his life. His bee-keeping, meanwhile, proves both a means of escape from the grim state of the world and a positive way of doing something about it. We could probably all do with some of that.'

Dixe Wills, *BBC Countryfile Magazine*

'Peppered with fascinating facts about bees, *Liquid Gold* is a compelling and entertaining insight into the life of the beekeeper. But it's much more than that. It's the story of a life at a crossroads when a series of random events sets the author off on a different, and more satisfying, path. It's a tale of friendship and fulfilment, stings and setbacks, successes and failures and finding meaning in midlife.'

WI Life

'[A] delightfully told story ... Wryly humorous with fascinating facts about bees, it charts the author's own mid-life story and the joys of making discoveries.'

Choice magazine

'The reader will learn plenty about bees and beekeeping from this book, although it is about as far from a manual as possible. *Liquid Gold* is a well observed delve into the hobbyist's desire to find what is important in life, no matter their age or preparedness.'

The Irish News

'[A] delightful exploration of the world of bees and their honey ... a hymn to the life-enhancing connection with the natural world that helped Morgan-Grenville reconcile himself to the fading of the light that is middle age.'

Country & Town House magazine

'Both humorous and emotionally affecting ... Morgan-Grenville's wry and thoughtful tale demonstrates why an item many take for granted should, in fact, be regarded as liquid gold.'

Publishers Weekly

By the same author

Liquid Gold: Bees and the Pursuit of Midlife Honey
(Icon, 2020)

Unlimited Overs (Quiller, 2019)

Not Out of the Woods (Bikeshed Books, 2018)

Not Out First Ball (Benefactum Press, 2013)

SHEARWATER

SHEARWATER

A Bird, An Ocean, and a Long Way Home

ROGER MORGAN-GRENVILLE

ICON

Published in the UK and USA in 2021
by Icon Books Ltd, Omnibus Business Centre,
39–41 North Road, London N7 9DP
email: info@iconbooks.com
www.iconbooks.com

Sold in the UK, Europe and Asia
by Faber & Faber Ltd, Bloomsbury House,
74–77 Great Russell Street,
London WC1B 3DA or their agents

Distributed in the UK, Europe and Asia
by Grantham Book Services, Trent Road,
Grantham NG31 7XQ

Distributed in the USA
by Publishers Group West,
1700 Fourth Street, Berkeley, CA 94710

Distributed in Canada by Publishers Group Canada,
76 Stafford Street, Unit 300
Toronto, Ontario M6J 2S1

Distributed in Australia and New Zealand
by Allen & Unwin Pty Ltd, PO Box 8500,
83 Alexander Street, Crows Nest, NSW 2065

Distributed in South Africa
by Jonathan Ball, Office B4, The District,
41 Sir Lowry Road, Woodstock 7925

Distributed in India by Penguin Books India,
7th Floor, Infinity Tower – C, DLF Cyber City,
Gurgaon 122002, Haryana

ISBN: 978-178578-720-1

Typeset in Sabon by Marie Doherty

Printed and bound in Great Britain by
Clays Ltd, Elcograf S.p.A.

CONTENTS

ABOUT THE AUTHOR

Roger Morgan-Grenville was a soldier in the Royal Green Jackets from 1978–86, serving all over the world. In 1984–85, he led the first expedition that successfully retraced Sir Ernest Shackleton's escape across the sub-Antarctic island of South Georgia. After leaving the British army, he worked in, and then ran, a small family company importing and selling kitchenware. In 2007–08, he helped to set up the charity Help for Heroes, and in 2020 he was a founding member of the conservation charity, Curlew Action. He jointly set up a roving cricket team in 1986 (The Winchester Hunters) and lives in West Sussex. This is his fifth book. His previous title, *Liquid Gold: Bees and the Pursuit of Midlife Honey*, is also published by Icon.

In memory of Elizabeth Freeman
1912–1986

*Dedicated to the small army of scientists, zoologists,
conservationists, policy-makers, wardens, charity
workers and volunteers whose work helps to explain our
wildlife to us, and ensures as best it can that it will still
be there for our children and grandchildren to cherish.*

A NOTE ON NAMES

Most of the names and places in this book are the real ones. Following seabirds is, however, generally a private activity, and I have occasionally protected the identities of the people I met on my travels by changing their names.

MAPS

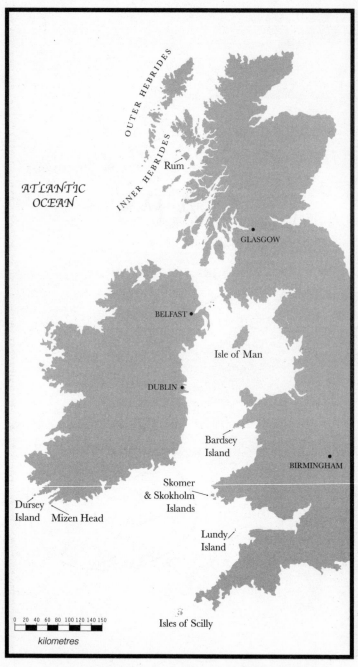

1. The western British Isles, showing main breeding sites
(Chapter 4) and other places mentioned in the book.

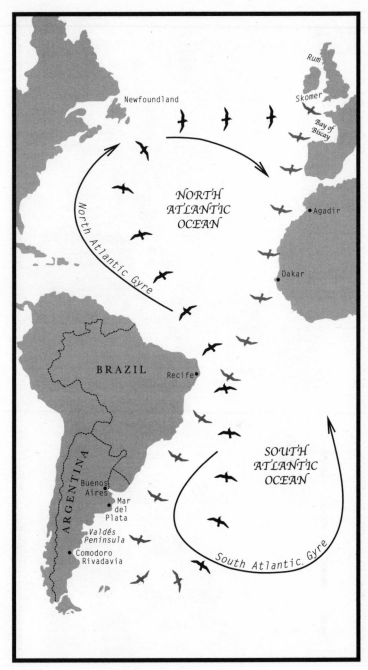

2. The Atlantic Ocean showing gyres and
migration routes (Chapter 7).

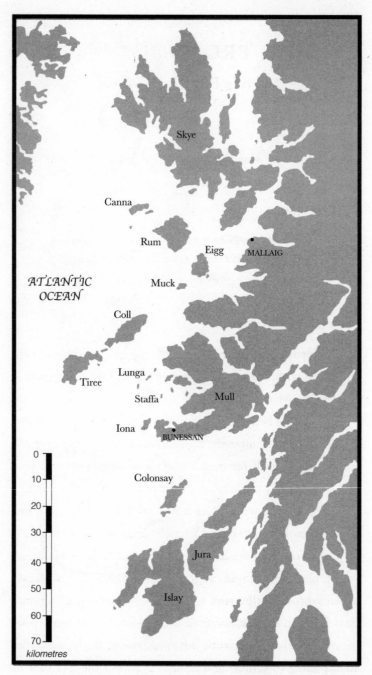

3. The Hebridean 'Small Islands' (Chapter II).

PROLOGUE
Wrong End of the World

May 2004, Tsu City, Japan

....

*From a certain point onward there is no longer any
turning back. That is the point that must be reached.*
FRANZ KAFKA

....

All bird species have occasional vagrants, members of the
clan who, for one reason or another, find themselves in
entirely the wrong place.

It might be because of fog or a strong and relentless wind;
it might be some fault in the bird's navigational wiring, or that it
simply found itself far out at sea, alighted on a passing ship
and then ended up wherever the ship happened to be going.

The vagrants we tend to see in the British Isles are often
blown over the 3,000-mile Atlantic Ocean by a prevailing gale,
or pushed up from the Sahara on the forward edge of a sand-
storm. Our most famous vagrant was probably 'Albert Ross',
a black-browed albatross who kept his lonely vigil around
Bass Rock in eastern Scotland on and off for 40 years from
the mid-1960s, his romantic advances among the gannets constantly fated to refusal and failure. It wasn't the fact that he

was 6,000 miles away from the northern end of his range that was astonishing – it was that he would have had to cross the equator and the tropics at some point to be here. Albatrosses need wind for their dynamic soaring flight and the tropics, as the Ancient Mariner found out to his cost, often don't have any.

One morning in mid-May 2004, a Japanese fisherman noticed a bird he didn't recognise just off the shoreline at Tsu City, a small industrial town a couple of hundred miles to the west of Tokyo. He was interested enough to bring it to the attention of one of Japan's most dedicated seabird experts, Hiroyuki Tanoi, who quickly and positively identified it as a Manx shearwater, photographing it for good measure to convince any doubters.

And doubters there absolutely would have been. For the Manx shearwater is a bird of the Atlantic, not the Pacific, breeding in the north of it from March to September, and then fishing under the Latin American sunshine for the rest of the year. Indeed, if you take the central point of the bird's southern range, somewhere off the coastal waters where Brazil, Argentina and Uruguay meet, and drill a line through to the opposite side of the planet, you will arrive in Tsu City, Japan. Meaning that this shearwater was a full 13,000 miles out of its range and on exactly the wrong side of the world, a distance that no vagrant in history has been recorded achieving. In fact, if you wanted to make a point, it was precisely in the one place that it really shouldn't have been, looking sleek and healthy, calmly fishing away as if it was off the Valdés Peninsula, or the Irish coast. Disorientated it may have been, but distressed it certainly wasn't.

To get to Japan, it would have had to do one of two things. Either it flew all the way down to Cape Horn, rounded it, and flew up the long western coast of South America until it got to Peru and allowed one of the prevailing winds to blow it across the small matter of the entire Pacific Ocean. Or it flew across the Atlantic, rounded the Cape of Good Hope, worked its way across the whole Indian Ocean until it got to Australia and then headed up through the Philippine Sea and thence to Japan. Every single mile in the wrong direction. Every single day, presumably, on its own. Maybe 40 or 50 days, fishing trips included.

It was May, and therefore the breeding season. And while there are other shearwaters on the Japanese coast, they are not ones with which a Manx could interbreed. So he or she (they never found out which) simply flew low over the beach houses at night making the eerie 'devil' call for which they are famous back in their British breeding grounds, looking for a mate or, worse still, searching for an imaginary chick. At one particular house, it kept striking the awning of the balcony and then landing, until the kindly owner took it in to protect it from the local cats, and released it to fly the next day.

The shearwater stuck around for two months until the night of July 13th when it disappeared for good, presumably working out simultaneously that raising a chick by the end of the season was unlikely, and that it had a bit of a commute ahead of it to get back home.

With no ring and no tracking information, we don't know exactly what happened to it; although, with a 92% survival rate between years for adult shearwaters, there is a reasonable chance that it at least got back to more familiar shores.

I tracked down Mr Tanoi, who turned out to remember every detail, and he sent me the photographs he had taken. He also told me that almost exactly seven years later, on July 16th 2011, another one had been identified from a ferry off the coast of Miyagi Prefecture, well up to the north of the country, but then no more.

We may not know any further details about that Tsu City bird, but we can guess with some certainty that she (if that is what we would like her to be) had once emerged from an egg inside a burrow on an island off the west coast of Britain and Ireland, and that, after 60 days or so, her parents quietly abandoned her. We know that ten days later, starving and having lost 30% of her body weight and preened her own downy feathers away, she would have stumbled out of her burrow one windy night, found the highest point in reasonable proximity, flapped her wings and risen up into the darkness. We know that from that point she would not have touched land again for four years or more, and that she would have ceaselessly roamed the oceans, possibly covering 40,000 miles each year.

We know that, on her first flight, a mix of genetic coding, smell, sight, sound, sun, stars and magnetic field would have guided her, not yet ten weeks old, down past the Bay of Biscay, past the dusty coast of Morocco and the Canary Islands, and down to Senegal, fishing from time to time, but mainly travelling. To put this in a human context, it is the equivalent of a four-month-old baby walking out of the house to make its own way in the world. We know that the shearwater would then have instinctively caught the helpful South Atlantic gyre, whose winds would have pushed her over to Brazil and then down the coast to Argentina, and the rich fishing grounds between there and the Falklands. We know that she would have gone through her rites of passage in the western Atlantic, laying down a mind map of the ocean and its fishing grounds, the better to prepare her for motherhood when changing hormones would drive her to the north-east one early spring. And that she would search for a mate and reclaim her burrow, probably no more than a few yards from where she was born, and thus continue the circle of life.

For as long as I can remember, I have chased her, more often in my imagination than out at sea. Schoolboy, soldier, trader, charity worker and writer: through all of those phases of my life she has been my metaphor for wilderness and adventure, always free, always out there, always just beyond reach.

The Manx shearwater is one of nature's near-perfect fliers. She is not a soaring bird of the heavens so much as a bustling presence low down on the salty horizons, a crosser of seascapes glimpsed from the stern of faraway vessels. From the structure and length of her wings to her ability to smell a potential meal ten miles upwind, from the desalination plant within her beak to her exquisitely complex navigational systems, she is a creature fully of air and water. Related to, but much smaller than the similar albatross, we know that she actually uses less energy flying through the air than she does resting on the water. Just as the camel has evolved as the supreme desert animal, so the shearwater has spent 120 million years perfecting the life of an ocean wanderer.

Out there, a few feet above the waves and beyond all human comforts, the shearwater is utterly at home.

This is the story of my 50-year search for her.

Part One

OUTWARD
BOUND

1. THE 83RD BIRD

1971, Isle of Mull

....

*There is no such thing as the pursuit of
happiness, but there is the discovery of joy.*
JOYCE GRENFELL

....

In the summer of 1971, Tuesdays were our puffin days.

Puffins were the natural history offerings of my childhood summers, on which it had been almost impossible to overindulge. Puffins were birdwatching made manifestly and childishly joyful, a pound of comic sweetness with sad clown's eyes, Charlie Chaplin walk and outsize colourful bill. Back then, when there was little talk of global warming, of struggling sand eel populations, or of decline, my sister and I just had an uncomplicated fascination with a creature that seemed more burlesque than seabird, and whose mannerisms somehow made us exquisitely happy.

We spent the middle part of each summer at my grand-mother's little Hebridean croft on the southern tip of the Isle of Mull, and at least once or twice each holiday she would get Callum the Boat to take us all over to the waters around Staffa to find them. Everyone on Mull seemed to have a handle back then, or at least they did to my grandmother: Angus the Coal, Glen the Store, Ian the Park. No one was entirely sure what Ian the Park did, but we used to find him in the late afternoons behind my grandmother's woodshed, passed out in a haze of cheap whisky, when she was paying him to sort out the fencing for her. In theory, he did the jobs around the place that she was no longer strong enough to do; in practice, he was a lame duck she couldn't bear to evict from under her wings. He knew it, she knew it, we knew it, and the knowledge of it changed nothing.

'Oh, he's got rather a lot on his mind,' she would tell my sister and me when we reported the state he was in, as if that explained everything.

Other children may have had more obviously exotic holi-days, but our trips to Mull were the integral hard landscaping in the garden of our young summers. The expression 'work hard, play hard' could have been invented for these stays, where morn-ings might be spent pulling ragwort from the stony field beyond the garden wall (a penny paid for proof of a dozen roots), carting sacks of seaweed up the rocky path to pile onto the vegetables, cutting tracks through the bracken in the hilly wood behind the house. But the payback for mornings of graft was the uncompro-mised availability of my grandmother for afternoon adventures, bundling along to favoured beaches to swim with the seals, climbing hills and settling in for tea with her eccentric array of widow friends dotted around the island. Often, these wanderings took us to the neighbouring holy island of Iona, where we would endlessly harvest the sea-smoothed white and green marble pebbles on St Columba's Bay, pebbles which even now sit on the terrace outside my Sussex kitchen door.

The tacit deal was that we understood our place in the pecking order – after the dogs but before the birds – and that we did our full share of the chores. She was more gang-leader than grandparent, as relentless at galvanising activity as she was a calm evening listener to childhood and teenage problems. Into the mix came a variety of bizarre activities that would now have any adventure training centre closed down on the spot – chainsawing logs without protection at the age of fourteen comes to mind – but we ate well, exercised massively and slept like happy corpses when each day was done. Those early summers of a life etch into memory their unforgettable colours: the blue hills beyond Bunessan, the speckled pink of the granite rock and the black-brown squelching ooze of the bog out there beyond the Ardfenaig sheep fank. And always the permanent but ever-changing presence of the surrounding sea and its raucous birds. Selective memory insists that it was just about always sunny, even when it wasn't, and that there were never midges, even when there were.

Sea and shorebirds, together with the relentless wind, that was the soundtrack of our times there, and it started on our very doorstep. The four-note monotone tutting of the resident great black-backed gulls, Laurel and Hardy, as they sat patiently on the cottage roof when nothing was happening, followed by their yelping long-calls when they spotted food. As children, there was nothing we weren't prepared to feed them when nobody else was looking; as gulls, there was nothing they would refuse. Gulls can live for over 25 years, so they eventually became as much of a fixture of the place as my grandmother, or Robin at the petrol pump on the way to Fionnphort, and we would politely ask after them in our letters, as if they were family. Out on the marshes between Loch Caol and Market Bay we would hear the trill of oystercatchers and the mew of the hunting buzzards. On the cliffs it would be the high notes of the golden eagle and then over on the evening sea-lochs, the maniacal cry of a single great northern diver. Best of all was that simultaneously life-enhancing and mournful call of the curlew, an expression of wilderness joy, or maybe an elegy for extinctions yet to come. Little by little, and without my ever knowing it, the sounds embedded themselves in a part of my soul that I was still too young to comprehend, or to access at will.

Generally, my parents would leave us, and her, to it, perhaps understanding the safety valve effect of a period of separation in a long summer school holiday. This meant that the adventure started with the allocation of the 'unaccompanied minor' badge on the BEA flight up from London, and only ended when my parents arrived for the last week of our stay. It was not that we didn't do adventures with them, it was just that they were different ones, with different rules and hierarchies. Mull simply gave my sister, my cousins and me the chance to go feral for a short period of time, and feral is what children do most naturally, if machinery and adults don't get to them first.

Chicken paste sandwiches in greaseproof paper, apples and Penguin biscuits were our staple diet for days out, chased down by whatever cordial my grandmother had recently made. Sometimes, she would take along a couple of cans of Tennent's lager to share with Callum, or whoever we were spending the day with. Depending on how she felt, she would let one of us drive her old Land Rover the three miles to Fionnphort Pier, while she sat in the passenger seat playing 'Clementine' or Tom Lehrer's 'We Will All Go Together When We Go' on a mouth organ she kept wrapped in a bandana in the glove compartment. For a boy whose coltish legs hardly reached the pedals, this illegal preface to the puffin day was so good as to be a tiny glimpse into the very backyard of heaven. The deal on both sides was that my father was never to know what we got up to when we were staying with her. Given that this regularly included being sent out to fish for mackerel for breakfast, without life-jackets, in her little boat on the adjacent sea loch, it was probably just as well.

'It'll be the puffins you'll be wanting to see again, I suppose,' Callum would sigh as we decanted ourselves and our kit from the pier onto his fishing boat. 'I'd say you're leaving it a wee bit late again this year.' It was his mournful catch-phrase, and he probably would have said it whenever we had come, and whatever we were looking for. Whatever else Callum had been put on earth for, it was not as a bringer of joy.

The essential problem was that schools down south, where we lived, didn't break up until well into July, by which time most of the pelagic* birds we were looking for were starting to

---

* A pelagic bird is one that spends all its life out at sea, other than when it comes to shore to breed.

head back out to sea. The best of the watching is gone by then, and what remains is down to luck and the prevailing weather.

I helped Callum cast off from the rusty iron ring on the pier, pleased to be publicly useful in such a physically undemanding way. The familiar smell of Callum's boat, a mixture of diesel oil, rope tar and old fish, managed to be both thrilling and slightly nauseating, and we were grateful that he chose to head up the tiny Bull Hole channel, between Mull and the skerry of Eilean nam Ban, rather than straight out to sea. It extended our shelter from the strong westerly breeze for another ten minutes, and delayed any possible seasickness. That wouldn't hit us till we passed the tiny white village of Kintra off our starboard bow, turned to port and reached the open sea.

That open sea was no stranger's thing, even to us who saw it so rarely. It was a huge part of why we were here, the 'ring of bright water' that surrounded our island, and our own, vast, private swimming pool. Twice a day it covered the silver sands that we ran on and, when it retreated, its fading water revealed the mussels, shrimps and sea anemones that kept us engaged hour after salt-encrusted hour. We grazed ourselves on its rocks as we slipped on the thick carpets of its ochre bladderwrack seaweed. It was the provider of mystery for us, as into it dived the vertical, laundry-white gannets, and out of it, if you were lucky, came mackerel and crabs to eat, otters to gaze upon and seals to swim with. The moods of the sea defined the day and the land we ran across. Journeys like the one we were on today supplemented the ferry crossings and the local fishing trips in my grandmother's sky-blue rowing boat, and gave the sea another, wilder context.

I sat up in the prow of the boat while the two adults exchanged news of local infidelities, and my sister chatted away with the friend she had brought up to Mull for the holiday. I had a tiny notebook-diary with a stubby pencil tucked into its spine for making notes of what I saw, the trick being to identify whatever I could for myself before having to ask for Callum's help. That was very definitely a last resort.

I have that little book still, the embryonic evidence that, even then, I was a captive to numbers. My looping, schoolboy hieroglyphics set out the order in which I saw different birds that late July Tuesday morning.

'Day 4233 of my life,' it begins, in which way it always began. Looking back at it, I suppose that, in a boyhood of only the most moderate achievements, just hanging around for nearly twelve years was a feat not to be underestimated. 'Weather: OK.'

'Great black-backed gull (lots); herring gull (ditto); arctic tern; oystercatcher; curlew; gannet (x4); cormorant (x2); heron; merganser (?); porpoise.' Every so often, the line of the pencil would jerk in a strange direction, driven by the sharp movements of the boat as she turned half to port to head out to Staffa, meeting head-on the first of the open sea swell.

I had a life list of 82 birds at the time, mostly seen in and around my parents' garden in Sussex, so these trips were always pregnant with the possibility of new additions. Such research as I was capable of here, namely a visiting birder from Holland whom I had met briefly in the Bunessan village stores the previous day, had suggested I might just get a black guillemot.

'There sits black guillemots on the water for you, maybe,' he had said mysteriously, as he bundled three cauliflowers and a two-day-old *Daily Mail* into his shopping bag. 'They were so for me two days since.'

Forty minutes later, we were nearing the dark and vertical mass of Staffa, its symmetrical bulk softening into its true natural irregularity as we approached. There were puffins, guillemots and razorbills bobbing around in the sea on the right side of the boat, which everyone else was watching from the starboard rail. I stayed on the other side watching gannets, and possibly just to make an adolescent point about not following the crowd or being predictable. Also, I knew that I would see things that the others wouldn't, which was the important thing, my lists being as much about competition as they were the true records of sightings.

That was the precise moment I saw it for the first time.

I can still hear my grandmother's voice in the background, telling Callum about something bad that had happened in Morocco earlier that week, a coup, and Callum, whose horizons in his latter years stretched genuinely no further than the sea around the Ross of Mull, saying enigmatically: 'Aye. Well, that will be the way folk do things down there.'

At first I thought it might be a gull or a fulmar as it raced towards me, but no, it was flying through the air in the wrong way, and far too fast. It seemed to be more in the sea than above it, three quick wing beats, glide, three wing beats, glide, jinking this way and that and always with one wing tip seeming to touch the waves. As it drew closer, I saw the torpedo-shaped body, the thin, sickle wings, the white underside and the dark top. When it passed directly behind the boat the end feathers of its right wing appeared to brush the very wave itself, and I knew for certain that I had never seen this bird before. I knew nothing of it, save that for a fleeting second, it had shone a beam of light into a world of wildness for me. I followed it round the stern of the boat, suddenly panicking that I would lose sight of it before I knew what it was, and miss the opportunity of a rarity.

'Callum!' I shouted, politeness thrown to the wind. 'What's that?'

'That's a shearwater,' he said slowly, once he had turned around and watched it for a second or two. And then, after a pause, 'She'll be a Manx shearwater. *Puffinus puffinus.*' He might not have known about coups in Morocco, but he knew the Latin name of every bird around the shores of his islands. 'She's a big wanderer, you know. One of the biggest of them all.' Over the years I had come to realise that all Callum's birds were 'she'.

I came back to sit next to him by the tiller.

'What do they ...' I couldn't think of the right word, so I just picked the first one that came into my head. 'What do they do?'

While he spoke, there were more shearwaters passing the back of his boat, heading back to some new fishery with a sense of purpose that seemed to elude the other seabirds.

'What do they do?' he repeated, pausing to see the effect of his words. 'I suppose they just fly and fly till there's no more ocean to fly over. These ones here will only be around for a few weeks and then ... next stop: the South Atlantic.'

'South Atlantic?!' I parroted in my astonishment. 'But that's across the equator!' It had never occurred to me that birds crossed the equator, a line that to my young brain was still somehow a physical one, let alone traversed half the globe.

'It is,' he said quietly. 'But I suppose that they don't really go there, because I don't think that they ever land there. They won't land until they get back here' – he nodded at the brooding bulk of Staffa – 'next spring.'

And on he went. He had been in the Merchant Navy after the war, and had plied those same seas himself. He talked of albatrosses and shrieking winds that bent the mast almost in half; the lonely days when you could see nothing but the horizon, and the green flash of the setting sun; the deep aquamarine of the troubled sea, and the whiteness of the tips of the dreaded greybeard waves crashing into and over the stern of his boat. I could see in my grandmother's eyes that his sea stories were losing nothing in the telling, but they spoke straight to the soul of a suggestible boy like me.

'Ah, those greybeards,' he said, his voice trailing off to some other time and place, like his pipe smoke wreathing into the sky above. 'You'll never forget your first one of those.'

And piece by piece, out there on a near-calm inland sea, he laid down for me the mosaic of the shearwater's world. He was in his element, and so was I. Exaggerations they may well have been, but he knew how to fire a boy up.

'That's where your bird over there goes when she's not here,' he finished. 'That's why she's always been my favourite. She's the size and weight of a little woodpigeon, you know, but she'll travel the world. I'm pleased to see the others, right enough, but she's the one that makes my heart sing.'

The prospect of this normally taciturn man's heart singing was one that intrigued me. I squinted southwards into the noonday glare and saw another shearwater beating its way into the wind, and then another, and then no more.

'Your bird.' That's what Callum had called it. My very own bird.

Little in my life dates back to an identifiable moment in time. Most of who I eventually became is the product of genetics and the thousand mundane developments that took place each hour of each day of my young life. So it is for all of us. But when that last shearwater beat its way across the wind, up towards its raft and then its night-time burrow among the wave-blasted, wind-sculpted revetements of Lunga, when the thoughts of Callum the Boat turned as they had from the workaday *now* to the heroic *then*, a switch had been thrown within me. From that moment on, the wilderness enticed me. No headland failed to summon me around it, no unclimbed hill allowed me to walk easily away, no pavement let me ignore what might lie beyond its last street-lit shadow. The wilderness now spoke to me of journeys without predictable endings, adventures deprived of certainty, like sentences without punctuation marks

That evening, I did what any eleven-year-old boy from the pre-internet age would have done, and scoured every shelf in my grandmother's sitting room for information about those wanderers of the ocean. Normally, evenings at Loch Caol were for canasta, a card game for which she regularly created new rules that acted for her benefit. 'Didn't you remember that one?' she would chuckle as she racked up the points towards yet another inevitable victory. But on the shearwater evening, recognising a significant moment in my young life, she spent suppertime kindling the flame that had been lit in my mind, giving me the confidence to believe that what I was feeling was something to be treasured, not ridiculed.

'It's better than the Rolling Stones,' she said in conclusion, as if that were reason enough to dedicate my life to them. 'All that long hair and drugs, I don't know!'

Deep down, I think she saw the shearwater as something that might draw me back to her island when teenage fancies might be beckoning me elsewhere. As I devoured the books that she found for me, whose grainy black-and-white images my mind's eye can still just about make out, I came to understand, with the brash certainty that only a child can truly muster, that a tiny part of me had been branded by that first shearwater.

For introducing me to a wildness not controllable by humans, Bird Number 83 trumped all the others. All the sparrows, chaffinches, gulls and hooded crows that were part of Ardfenaig garden life were to a large extent predictable – not, as with the shearwater, birds that would emerge from, and recede back into, their wild ocean home. On reflection, there was nothing unusual in this: my grandmother's trick was to let the wild glories of her world present themselves to you according to their own natural rhythm, and not to the dictates of any human plan.

If that shearwater happened to have spoken to me, it had done so very much on its own terms.

2. DIOMEDES' SECRET

October 1984,
53.1 Degrees South, 41.4 Degrees West

....

It seems to me that we all look at nature too much,
and live with her too little. I discern great sanity
in the Greek attitude. They never chattered about
sunsets, or discussed whether the shadows on the
lawn were really mauve or not. But they saw that the
sea was for the swimmer, and the sand for the feet
of the runner. They loved the trees for the shadows
they cast, and the forest for its silence at noon.

Oscar Wilde

....

It was exactly how it should have been, a beautiful moment
paid for entirely by the taxpayer.

I was a dozen or so years older than I had been on that day
off Staffa, and once again in a boat. My potentially grateful
nation had sent me down to the sub-Antarctic island of South

Georgia for five months in the wake of the Falklands War, to do my bit to keep it once more in British hands. One invasion was embarrassment enough for a lifetime, they told us as we sailed off from Port Stanley on RFA *Sir Lancelot*,* and, to ensure we saw off anyone else thinking of giving it a go, they gave us a cargo of more explosives and pyrotechnics than even our wildest young dreams had allowed for. In a military career where the most likely postings were to the dull north German plains or the unhappy streets of West Belfast, to be heading for the land of ice, of wilderness and of Ernest Shackleton was adventure writ large, and we knew it.

The journey out from England had taken twenty tedious days and had involved just about every form of transport yet developed by humanity, including plane, helicopter, coach, car, liner, launch and foot. A touch of complexity had been added by an unscheduled landing in Senegal on the way down to Ascension Island, which meant that we must have been the only Arctic warfare troops in the world taking anti-malaria tablets for six weeks among the icebergs. Seasickness was taking a fearful toll on my platoon on the last leg from Port Stanley to Grytviken, across the exposed sea-wastes of the Southern Ocean. Right now, most of the soldiers were lying below deck in varying states of physical anguish, still 200 miles west of our destination, and a source of sadistic pleasure to the ship's crew in exactly inverse proportion to their own well-being.

....

* Twin of the ill-fated RFA *Sir Galahad*, and a 5,000-ton flat-bottomed tub.

'She rolls a bit, what with her flat bottom and all that,' said the skipper rather too cheerfully for my liking, lighting his pipe and gazing out at the mountainous lines of swell rolling in from our starboard quarter. 'So it's nice that it's calm for you lot.' The sickly sweet smell of the pipe smoke, the after-effects of the nameless pie I had eaten for supper and the muffled sound of our medic vomiting into the abyss somewhere close by all conspired to defeat the last of my own stoicism, and I lumbered wordlessly from the bridge to stand outside at the rear of the ship, listen to the thrum of the twin diesel engines and breathe in the raw power of nature. Death, it occurred to me, was only marginally worse than what I was starting to go through, and I stared into the vacant greyness of the Scotia Sea wondering idly how cold, how bad it really would be if I slipped in, and who might nibble at me as I made my uncomplaining way to the bottom.

But once we were on the island, I thought to myself, we would be all right. Utterly on our own, joyfully on dry land, we would be some of the most remote soldiers on the planet. Thirty-three infantrymen with a small complement of cooks, engineers, medics and signallers to keep us fed, heated, healthy and in touch; young enough to feel invincible, but smart enough to understand that we probably weren't. Ice warriors, fantasists, poets, body-builders and wildlife observers, we would be living the soldier's ultimate dream of being 950 miles away from the next link up in the chain of command. Every six weeks or so a ship would call in to see how we were getting on and check that we were doing the important stuff, like cleaning our rifles and shaving; the intervals between visits would be punctuated by a low fortnightly fly-by from an RAF C130, whose crew would unceremoniously lob out of its rear cargo door a vast waterproof bag containing fresh food, instructions and mail, which we would duly retrieve by inflatable boat from among the icebergs in our bay. Otherwise, we would spend our time climbing on glaciers, reading books and looking as fierce as our youthful complexions allowed, the better to deter any lurking invaders.

As for the neighbourhood we were moving into, our fellow residents would simply be the five million or so penguins on the island, half a million or more elephant seals and all the assorted seabirds that had not yet evolved a reason to fear the presence of humans. It was certainly going to be a long way from the flat, corvid world of Salisbury Plain, from where we had set off three weeks before. For a young man partly raised on the cry and the folklore of the seabird, it was a wonderful thing to be asked to go and do, an enthusiasm I had hidden as well as I could during the tearful goodbyes at home.

Birds had drifted in and out of my life over the last dozen years since that afternoon off Staffa, normally 'in' while I was on Mull or on the coast, and 'out' while I was anywhere else. Watching birds also tended to be something I fell back on when I was down and then ignored when I was cheerful, which I was most of the time. Every now and again, I would drag my tangled teenage confusions along with me on some long-distance footpath, watching choughs churning and spilling over the cliff edges, all the while wondering self-indulgently whether I should eventually be a soldier, poet, tycoon or armchair anarchist. Thus, depending on whether it was Byron or Bonaparte who had turned up on the day, did I watch birds from a standpoint of either romantic idealism or detached superiority, before heading to a local pub and pretending, as I downed my beer, that I hadn't been privately educated. Teenage can be complicated like that.

Crucially, birding was also what I shared with my father, who had an accountant's fastidiousness about his claims and his note-keeping. When communication was fractious between us, which it quite often was in those years on the cusp of my adulthood, he would use the offer of a bird trip to allow calm to seep back into our relationship. After all, it's hard to argue about life if you are both lying on the ground trying to work out if that thing browsing by those rocks is a Temminck's or a little stint.

I kept a list of the birds that I had seen from on board the MV *Keren*,* the boat that took us from Ascension Island to Port Stanley, and the first lengthy sea journey I had ever made. Bird Number 83 is on it, as are great and sooty shearwaters, enormous cousins of the Manx, the latter of which ranges into every ocean on earth. But there had been no gasp of recognition, no thrill of reunion, just a routine and dutiful logging of a fact into a misused military notebook on the back of a commandeered liner. My role was to protect the outer reaches of

....

* Ships have many lives. Built as a Channel car ferry, she briefly earned the title 'HMS' in the Falklands War, when she was used, among other things, to repatriate Argentine prisoners. After plying the route between Ascension Island and the Falklands as a troopship, she went back to being a Channel ferry, before ending her days as a carrier for Sudanese pilgrims to Mecca and finally being scrapped in 2009 in India. *Sir Lancelot* was scrapped in India the same year.

what was left of my nation's empire, not to return to a childish enthusiasm.

A week later, on the ship from Stanley to South Georgia, it took a single moment in time to change me back for ever.

———

As the minutes passed out there on the deck and my core temperature plummeted, I started to regain some sense of equilibrium, and by way of diversion re-read my share of the mail that had been delivered to us at Port Stanley two evenings before. The final one of these was from my grandmother, typed and corrected by her rheumatic Hebridean hands on an old Smith Corona typewriter, back there in her whitewashed croft on the Ross of Mull. I always read hers last.

'Not much going on here. Ian the Park has been drunk for a week, and I am therefore beginning to wonder if I shall ever get my raspberry cage mended in time for next year's crop. A young couple rolled their car off the cliff road at Gribun and Annie M at Kintra said that "when they woke up in the morning, they were all cold". Other than that, just the normal infidelities and howling winds.'

The letter finished with an uncharacteristic intercession for my personal safety.

'I will pray nightly to St Jude (the patron saint of lost causes) that you don't fall down too many crevasses while you're on your mission. However, if you do, I am told that some previous record of prayer on your own part would be quite useful, too, plus the more tangible help of crampons.

'And think of it not as work but as a privileged adventure. Keep safe, don't complain and, above all, have fun. I will send you some whisky for Christmas if your generals don't find it first.'

Then there was a postscript to say that she had included in the envelope a 1917 George V penny that she had found in her coin drawer, to remind me of the year that Ernest Shackleton had made the first crossing of the island. 'Keep it in your pocket,' she had added, 'and it might just make you more adventurous, too, and keep you safe.' In a way, it did both, as four months later a group of us retraced the explorer's epic crossing of the island at the end of his escape from the Antarctic ice.

While finishing the letter, I had developed a vague sense that I was being watched and, for a second, couldn't think by whom, or from where. It was only when I folded the letter back into its envelope and looked southwards over the starboard rail into the vast grey acreage of emptiness beyond that I noticed a shadow in the corner of my left eye. I turned to look more closely at it.

I knew enough about seabirds to understand without any hesitation that it was a wandering albatross, my first. Most seabirds are predominantly white, especially below, but there is a glowing purity of whiteness about the wanderer that makes identification simple, even from a distance. It had taken a long time, a dozen years, for his flight to intersect with mine.

Given the folkloric expectation of a 'first albatross' to change the life of even the most part-time birder, I was initially calm. It was a major tick on the life list for sure, like one of the big five in an African game reserve, but no more than that. Almost an anti-climax. A large seagull, in fact.

But then it started to dawn on me that the bird I was looking at was still two football pitches' distance away from me, working his* silent way across the wind towards the ship, growing with every twitch of his wings until he took up station a few yards above and astern of where I was standing, alert for what we might disturb, or discharge. Albatrosses generally whiten with age, and his spectral brilliance suggested that he was a veteran of maybe 30 years, with perhaps five million miles behind him. He was vast, other-worldly, elegant, a creature fully of the wind, an envoy from the islets and tidal wastes of the Scotia Sea. His wingspan was out of all proportion to any bird I had ever seen. The 'large seagull' had transformed before my eyes into the giant manifestation of some lost childhood dream. I had never seen anything so beautiful, or so intensely personal. I think I gasped and, for an instant, held my breath lest some noise be the cause of his early disappearance. No picture from my childhood could have conveyed the enormous stillness of his shearing body, the seeming fragility of those long glider's wings, or the effortless speed with which he tracked alongside the fifteen knots of our progress. I could clearly see his massive head scanning from side to side, and imagine the depths beyond his fathomless eye. Bit by bit, every fragment of every childish legend I had ever held for this bird was made manifest for me.

....

* And a 'he' it would have been. Females tend to circle the globe well to the north of the boys.

For a second, nothing else existed, and how could it? For a boy who had once learned to recite the whole of the *Ancient Mariner* by heart,* and had thrilled to Herman Melville's *Moby-Dick* from the warmth of his Sussex bed, this was the end point of all the natural world that I had wanted to see while I was here. Just to intersect our lives on this precise coordinate of the Southern Ocean was a gift beyond privilege. I wanted both to share the moment with someone else and to keep it utterly to myself.

Corporal Mayer broke the spell by staggering onto the deck like a vision of Banquo's ghost, with the grim air of someone who wanted a quick release from his sufferings.

'Whose stupid idea was this?' he asked. I considered suggesting that the blame probably lay with General Galtieri or Margaret Thatcher, depending on whose side you were on, but thought better of it.

'Just look at it,' I said instead, with a biblical but ill-judged intensity as he pulled up alongside. I pointed to the bird above. 'That's a wandering albatross. They say that you'll never forget your first albatross.' To my mind, this was a cunning way of taking his mind off just how awful he felt, but I quickly saw that it hadn't worked.

'They say that, do they?', he muttered after a minute of silence. 'Well, you know what I say to them, with respect and all that?'

....

* Ironically, there is no evidence that people thought killing albatrosses was unlucky before Coleridge wrote his poem, and they were regularly shot and eaten by sailors. Through his poem, Coleridge may even unwittingly have kick-started marine conservation.

But I never found out. The effort of even saying those eighteen words had done for him, and he lurched off to the leeward rail to further enrich the Southern Ocean with the processed waste of a forgotten military meal.

When I looked up, my albatross had gone, shearing away into the white-flecked folds and re-folds of the endless seascape, perhaps back to its remote Annenkov Island fastnesses. But, in those seconds, I had been reunited with the raw emotion of a single moment in time exactly half my life earlier and 8,000 miles further north. For a minute or two, it was so powerful that it was almost a physical presence within me.

I felt almost comically far from home, further than I had ever been in my 24 years; but, for a reason I couldn't immediately identify, those minutes with the wandering albatross persuaded me that I had been here all my life. They also gently set a question into my mind that spent another 30 years running around within it, returning in pulses whenever I spent time by the sea.

'What happens with those ocean birds when they go out of sight?'

Like a wildflower seed buried in a desert, the thought lay dormant but alive inside me.

3. FANTASY RABBIT HOLES

July

....

*I am glad that I will not be young in
a future without wilderness.*
ALDO LEOPOLD, FATHER OF
AMERICAN CONSERVATION

....

Halfway through the first solo week I ever spent with my grandmother at her cottage, she wandered into my bedroom at five o'clock one morning, brandishing a loaded shotgun.

Thirteen-year-old boys sleep deep and long as a rule, and it took my adolescent brain quite some time to put the pieces together and come up with confirmation that, despite appearances, this probably wasn't life-threatening. Or not immediately so.

'There's a rabbit in among the carrots,' she said, as if we had been casually chatting for hours and she was doing no more than changing the subject. 'My shoulder isn't strong enough any more, so I'm afraid you'll have to shoot it for me.' She handed me the gun as I stumbled from bed, explaining casually as she did so that the safety catch was 'a bit iffy' these days.

By the time I had got down to the vegetable garden in my pyjamas and dew-soaked feet, making as much noise as I could, the rabbit had bolted, and with it a gut-full of her heirloom carrots. She was not good at hiding her disappointment when events didn't go her way, and things between us were on the monosyllabic side until she suddenly asked brightly at lunchtime what I would most like to do with my afternoon. My own grievous sins had been put into context by the fact of Ian the Park having destroyed her precious chainsaw the day before by running it without oil until it coughed, seized and died. Having a sleep, which was what I really wanted, wasn't an option; that would be like suggesting to her that we went off to rob the bank in Tobermory, only less fun.

'Can we go to Carsaig and see what's there?' I asked. We both knew what would be there: eagles in numbers on the thermals around those southern cliffs, stinking feral goats down by the seashore to chuckle at, and any amount of wildlife for her arthritic retriever to go through the motions of chasing. Part of my calculation was also that there was no way she would allow this trip to finish without a visit to the cake shelf at the Pennyghael Stores on the way home: in the equation of my young life, the promise of cakes equalled or exceeded most of the onerous things that I might be asked to do to earn them. So sometimes distanced, sometimes brought closer by the 50 years between us, we sped along the single-track road in her Land Rover, talking of the recent developing violence in Belfast.

She wore her politics on her sleeve, my grandmother, making no patronising allowances for the age of her audience, and it was with a sense of some relief on my part that we eventually parked up and walked our way to the moorland meadow above the sea cliffs. After all, animated political discourse is a hard trick to pull off for an elderly committed smoker with a heart condition, going steeply uphill and in single file.

There we found an adder on a path through the bracken, fully three feet long and lying half-coiled in the sun, and I smiled briefly at the notion that her only concern was for the dog, not the grandchild, whose job, in her view, was to do his own risk assessments and stay clear of trouble. After a while, we half sat, half lay down in the scented comfort of a heather ledge eating melting Penguin biscuits, overlooking the sea and observing what flew around us.

'That's more like it,' she said with a sigh of content, almost as if what had gone before had somehow displeased her. I toyed with asking her whether this was because, as it would have been for me, she only really found satisfaction in places other people couldn't or wouldn't go to, but I let it pass.

Twenty miles or so to our south was the three-papped outline of Jura, and in between the islands a blue sky-full of seabirds over a bright sea full of movement. Cormorants, all purpose and speed, commuted horizontally across the surface of the water while brilliant white gannets plunged into it vertically. And everywhere, the raucous cries of the omnipresent gulls. This was the birds' world, and not ours; we were there as tolerated guests.

'What do you think of when you see them?' she asked me, watching the fulmars wheeling around their cliff-top cities and flying off out to their fishing grounds. I didn't know, or couldn't say, and so immediately reversed the question back to her.

'Wilderness,' she said straight away; and then, so quietly that I almost lost the words in the breeze, 'and freedom.'

———

Forty-five summers later, Bird Number 83 came back into my life.

That inherited search for wilderness had beckoned my wife, Caroline, and me to 'The Small Isles' of Muck, Canna, Eigg and Rum on a late summer break to walk and climb our way around them.

Everyone has a direction that they naturally look towards, and mine is north. The same polarity had drawn me north-wards each year, and then west, as often as life allowed it. From earliest childhood, the journey up the A6, the A74 and the A82, Alasdair Maclean's 'Rainbow Road',* was one that I could navigate in my sleep. It was punctuated by familiar waymarks at every turn: Lancaster (halfway there, once you had spotted the dome of the Ashton Memorial Building on your left-hand side); Lockerbie (picnic lunch of ham sandwiches, always with midges, normally in the rain); the Rest and Be Thankful Pass (first view of the sea); and then Oban itself (gateway to the islands, with its Coliseum and red-funnelled ferry). As I got older, I found that I would venture further north, often alone,

....

* From Maclean's *Night Falls on Ardnamurchan*. Required reading for anyone trying to connect with their inner crofter.

initially summoned by the love of place and by reading books like *A Spade Among the Rushes* and *The Flight of the Heron*: Kyle of Lochalsh, Plockton, Lochinver, Kinlochbervie, ever northwards I went until one summer I finally found myself standing at Muckle Flugga Point* trying to explain to my young and not particularly interested children how great skuas forced other seabirds to disgorge what they had caught. Since then, the children had flown the nest, so these slow-paced, cheap journeys of discovery were now back on the menu.

'It's not exactly Corfu,' Caroline had said cheerfully as our ferry set out from Mallaig in the drizzle. 'But at least I've got the midges to look forward to once this all stops.' She was right, it wasn't her sun-drenched dream, but this break was my choice by rotation. She would get Venice soon enough. She would get collegiate sympathy from me, possibly even a plumped-up sleeping bag, but she wouldn't expect an apology. Apologies were only due if the holiday had been mis-sold, its promised treats exaggerated by the person booking it, and I definitely hadn't done that.

Three days later, we had hitched a lift on a boat from Muck to Rum, and were scanning the seas around us in the sunshine for signs of the orca that one of us thought we had seen a few minutes back. My own watch was from the port rail, just as it had been with Callum the Boat 47 years earlier. Looking back at it now, I realise that I had probably already seen other shearwaters on the trip, but this one came from exactly the same angle and height as my first-ever Manxie, unlocking some

----

* The northernmost point of Great Britain.

image etched deep in my subconscious, and bringing in its wake an overwhelming sense of familiarity. The boat was headed in the same direction as Callum's had been, just east of north, and both were late-morning trips, which meant that even the position of the sun and the intensity of light was similar. There was no possible questioning what it was.

And so it was that, from the middle distance, the shearwater flew back into my life, 17,532 days after its predecessor.

This time it stayed.

I still remembered enough about shearwaters to know that there was a chance, even if a mathematically small one, that this could have been the very same bird as I had seen back in 1971, on the basis of longevity of the species and of our both being in the same part of the world. After all, a Northern Irish Manx shearwater that had once been ringed as an adult (meaning that it was already more than five years old at that point) in the year Everest was conquered, was re-trapped exactly 50 years later just after the Second Gulf War. That bird must have been at least 55 years old, a good deal older than mine would need to be. Anyway, just about any shearwater breeding in Britain could reasonably find itself fishing in these waters. Like their albatross cousins down in the windswept southern oceans, they live long and travel far. Multiplying the number of years they can live by the number of miles that their annual migrations and fishing trips must inevitably comprise, we reach a figure of two to three million miles for the longest-lived of them. Possibly much more.

The Manx shearwater lives out its British breeding season in the not unwelcome shadow of the more celebrated puffin.

Thus, every accessible puffin colony becomes a visitor hotspot for three months of each summer, while the unremarkable burrow a little bit further up the hill containing the far more remarkable shearwater remains as silent in the daytime as a Trappist supper, the unfairness further compounded by the sea parrot, as it always used to be known, having also stolen the 'puffin' name. After all, *Puffinus puffinus* was once a puffin too.

But, as I would come to learn, it is the shearwater's reliable anonymity as much as any other factor that has helped it to prosper.

⌒

At its very simplest, the Manx shearwater is a small seabird that eats fish and nests in a burrow.

In fact, armed only with that piece of information, you know more about it than around 95% of the population. Like most seabirds, it is dark on top (camouflage from potential predators looking downwards) and light below (camouflage against the sky from potential meals looking up). But there the similarities stop. It only operates on land at dead of night and makes a 20,000-mile round trip each year to the oceans around southern Brazil and Argentina. Unless you've gone looking for it, or know your birds, the chances are you have not seen one. Other than to breed, it will never touch the ground again once it has left it for the first time. Estimating seabird numbers is by its nature an inexact science, but it's likely that there are around one and a half million of them alive at any one time. With that in mind, it's surprising that the accepted collective noun for shearwaters is an 'improbability';* if you go to the right places to find them, and at the right time of day, there is nothing improbable about the Manx shearwater.

To see that shearwater fly in the Sound of Rum was to watch something self-evidently in its element, the coastal sighting of a consummate ocean traveller. Other birds that we watched off the back of the boat that day – puffins, guillemots, razorbills – had to beat their wings continually to stay in the air, and therefore had a much higher 'cost of travel' which, in turn, would restrict their migration possibilities to the coastal waters of the North Atlantic. You could even argue that the latter three are each somewhere on a journey back towards flightlessness, like the penguins and great auks before them, while the shearwater is heading in the opposite direction.† Meanwhile, the cormorant is all bustle and intent, the Arctic tern all delicate deflections, while the muscular elegance of the gannet in flight is restricted to relatively short expeditions, punctuated by spectacular – and sometimes fatal – dives.‡

....

* *A Conspiracy of Ravens*, Bill Oddie (Bodleian Library, 2014). In which we also learn that we have bazaars of guillemots, circuses of puffins and strops of razorbills.

† You also might have a tough time arguing it. I put this theory to about seven academics over the next year, and only one of them – the one who had proposed it to me in the first place – agreed.

‡ For many years it was assumed that gannets went blind on account of years of open-eyed plunge dives, and starved to death as a result. The prosaic truth, according to a recent New Zealand study, is that they are prone to fatal head and neck injuries from crashing into each other while after the same fish. The gannet has a nictitating membrane that closes across the eye at the instant of impact, to protect it from damage.

I found myself remembering what Callum the Boat had said that day off Staffa nearly half a century before, about the young shearwater launching itself off some island one September night as its final act of fledging, hurling itself into the dark, and not touching land again for three years, and, for a split second, I understood. Why would a seabird touch land if it didn't have to? Out at sea there were no predators, no threat other than starvation and extreme weather. On land it was a different matter, and you could count a dozen species that would kill an infant seabird round these parts and still not have included half of them. A life at sea was a pretty good option.

I knew subliminally that they would be fledging pretty soon, and then all gone.

After that, all was miracles.

———⟋———

The following day, I was stuck fast halfway up a perilously steep grassy bank 2,000 feet up, above one cliff and below another, wondering how my day had managed to go so spectacularly wrong.

The good weather had held when we arrived on Rum, which meant that Caroline could get on with her painting down in the valley, and I was free to hoist a pack on my back and spend my daytimes tramping the high ridges of the Rum Cuillins, the ultimate antidote to my sedentary, southern life. I also had a comical notion that I could use my long-redundant military fieldcraft skills to get close up to Britain's largest herd of red deer, and take some memorable photographs.

The south of the island is studded with a horseshoe of rocky peaks between 2,000 and 2,500 feet high, each one technically without challenge but still steep and rugged enough to require kit and planning, and the occasional head for heights. It was to the two most prominent of these, Askival and Hallival, that I headed off on my first full day. As the morning had worn on, a thick band of cloud had settled on Hallival, just at the point that the path I was on steepened dramatically and turned into, first, a deer path and then no path at all. By the time I noticed what had happened, I had already broken the cardinal rule of climbing by not having a workable back-out option, and was now faced with the uncomfortable choice of climbing on into the steepening unknown, or clambering down what had become a death trap of slippery grass and sharp rocks ending in a small cliff, both options in nil visibility. 'Idiotic bird-watcher falls off Scottish mountain', the tragic headline might run in Mallaig's *West Word* news sheet, 'Final words reported as "Don't worry. I know what I'm doing."'

Half scared, and half excited by a ridiculous situation that was entirely of my own making, I took the middle-aged option of sitting astride a convenient rock for a while, chewing on a sandwich and waiting for a good idea to present itself, while the thickening cloud swirled around and occasional falling stones signalled the presence of more sure-footed animals somewhere above me. Far below, I could hear the cry of the invisible gulls down on the lee shore of the island, not in a comforting way, but in a way that simply emphasised how high up and exposed I was. All around me were high-altitude rabbit holes, the petite excavations of what was obviously a smaller, hardier northern breed than the ones I was used to in the Weald of Sussex.

Then I remembered what the little guide to the island on the bedside table at our bed and breakfast had said: 'There are no rabbits on Rum.'

'You could fool me,' I thought. 'You're just not looking in the right place. They're everywhere.' I thought about it a bit further, until something slotted into place. For the leaflet then goes on: 'The architects of the burrows will become apparent if you stay on the Cuillin until well after dark. This is when strange and eerie noises come from the burrows, and hundreds of black and white shapes whoosh low overhead.'[1] My current predicament gave me every chance of still being on the hillside well after dark to see all this for myself, but I was equally keen not to become an incompetent mountain rescue statistic, and so I crawled over to the nearest burrow, saw the tell-tale signs of little flecks of grey down at its entrance, and put my ear right over the hole.

As I lay there, a sound filtered out, almost too faint and too high to register on hearing badly compromised by years of military gunfire, and I slowly started to tune in to a series of infant cheeps, tiny noises that suggested I was expected to be the deliverer of a fish supper to the resident chick within. Unwittingly, I had stumbled across, and right into the heart of, one of the largest and highest-altitude shearwater breeding grounds in the world.* Yesterday out in the Sound of Rum, I had seen those birds only as elegant passers-by in the middle

....

* The Hutton's shearwater probably nests higher up, in New Zealand.

distance, and had been an abstract part of a background scene to them, much as they had been to me. Today, I was accidentally within touching distance of their children.

In the excitement of finding out what I was in the middle of, I had completely forgotten my predicament. I got up from my rock and started to wander around the colony, finding similar holes every few feet; holes in the grass and in the places where the grass bordered the rocks; holes in between boulders, and in the tiny scree runs; holes above, below and alongside me.

They sometimes call these colonies 'shearwater lawns',* bringing to mind exquisite greens in some pristine home counties village, not a bustling, underground vertical city 2,000 feet up in the clouds between two cliffs on a Scottish island.

At first sight, it seemed strange to me that a seabird would want to make its marital home high up on a mountainside that was at least a mile and a half from the nearest bit of coast, but the more I thought about it, the more I understood. Rum was once a supervolcano, and it has taken 60 million years of glacial and other forms of erosion to wear it down to the shape and form it is now, leaving a cap of fast-drying, fine-grained sandstone on top of the layered lava intrusion that happens to be close to ideal for a shearwater. In short, the digging is easy, and the surrounding gravel is both soft and fast-draining. Dig-ability and drainage are to shearwaters what good transport links and excellent secondary schools are to human house buyers. A lack of predators, by the same token, is their version

* The vivid green of the lawns is, of course, the result of centuries of rich, fish-centred shearwater droppings.

of safe streets: most rats don't wander that far up the hill, and gulls and skuas, the other enthusiastic predators, generally venture no higher than 30 metres or so above the sea.[2] And, as I was to discover, many birds are genetically programmed to come back to the same place, often the same few square metres, as they were born: just about every adult bird in this colony of 40,000 or so, no matter how old, was probably born here.

Quite how the first birds worked out that this was a good spot for a colony has defeated research, although a lengthy process of trial and error seems a probability; presumably there were previous generations who dented their beaks and shredded their feet trying to excavate the granite immediately below, gradually coming to the conclusion that it simply wasn't working. When the evolutionary music paused, and all the other oceanic birds were sitting on wet and windswept stacks and sea-cliffs waiting for the next attack by a skua or a great black-backed gull, the infant shearwater was safe and sound a few feet inside a burrow, waiting for its next meal by putting its feet up and relaxing on a soft bed of moss and grass. Charles Darwin probably didn't articulate the sentiment, but sometimes it seems that natural selection is kinder to some species than others.

Eventually, taking advantage of a small break in the clouds, I clambered on upwards and was soon standing by the cairn at the summit of Hallival, still with burrows more or less all around me. As had happened so often in my half-century of following wildlife, what I had hoped and planned to see – the red deer and the golden eagles – had been overshadowed and then eclipsed by what I had actually found. By the time I got back down to the village a couple of hours later, the mental sifting process had shed everything else, leaving only shearwaters.

Sometimes the biggest decisions are the simplest ones, because they are made *for* us, not *by* us. I didn't realise it at the time, but from that small start, or re-start, the shearwater would come to dominate my thoughts and plans for the following year.

On the boat back to Mallaig a few days later, at the end of our trip, I had wilderness very much on my mind. To look up to an unclimbed mountain, to stare over a wild ocean, was to ignite in me a small pilot light of longing, powerful enough to bring me back to the outer edges of wildness year after year, but never quite strong enough to fire up the main boiler and throw myself deeper into it. Things that humans created or did could have a beauty of their own, of course, but to me they could never be equal to what was already here before man learned simultaneously to create and destroy. In nature, it seemed, to learn about one species simply drew the curtain back on twenty more, and twenty more again after that, and on all the environments they passed through.

Looking aft of the ferry, the sea was its normal melee of seabirds about their business. It frustrated me that these coastal waters were the only intersecting arc of the Venn diagram between their lives and mine, the only opportunity I had to be near them. Beyond that, I had as much awareness of the pelagic majority of their lives as they had of my National Insurance number. In a month or so, most of them would be gone, travelling beyond the world I knew into that vortex of winds and waves that Callum would once have been familiar with. They would be gone, the puffins, guillemots, razorbills and auks, and bringing up the rear would be those Manx shearwater chicks at the top of Hallival, perhaps a full two months after the first puffins had flown. Their temporary disappearance was inevitable, of course, but what surprised me was how much their coming absence affected me. In a world of intractable problems and idiot leaders doing their best to make them even more insoluble, the biggest issue on my own mind was seabird separation anxiety. I needed to get out more, it was clear, but the question was, to where?

I watched the shearwaters flying behind the ferry, studying them intently through the binoculars. They are, in many ways, the ultimate flying machines, and it's from their flight that they take their name – 'shearing' the water with a fractional contact from their wingtip – and their extraordinary journeying ability. 'Scalpel blades in the wind' was how Adam Nicolson described them to me a year later, and I still can't improve on that notion.

No two bird species fly exactly the same, and all of bird flight is some sort of a compromise. Flying is a desirable activity, in that it allows for specialist migratory and feeding activities, but also a costly one, as the act of getting into and remaining in the air has a high energy cost (the 'metabolic price'). The compromise is generally based on how the bird is to get its food, and how far and fast it has to travel to get there, and also to breed. The tiny Allen's hummingbird, for example, beating its wings 50 times per second while hovering in front of a flower, needs a very different wing design to the bar-headed goose, flying six miles up over the high Himalayas; just as the Ruppell's griffon vulture, which soars on thermals above the African plains waiting to spot a meal, would fare dismally manoeuvring itself on a sixpence, chasing flies above a busy Italian piazza, like the European swift does. The inputs into flight in reverse order of importance, if you are an ocean-going seabird, are manoeuvrability, speed, lift, endurance and soaring. The shearwater wing has evolved to enable what is called 'dynamic' soaring, a sequence of upwind climbs and downwind dives and glides that take advantage of the range of different air pressures immediately above the sea.[3] This is what the great bird artist Archibald Thorburn referred to in his 1916 *British Birds* as 'when fairly on the wing they fly with great speed, and follow each other as they sweep onwards in undulating curves'. And Thorburn generally got it right.

Its wings are shorter than its cousin the albatross (so that it can operate under water for short periods, which the albatross doesn't have to), but longer than the tiny storm petrel (who flies in a different way). In whatever other manner the shearwater makes itself a challenging bird to follow and observe, and there are many, you generally never have to look more than a few metres in the air to see them. And, while you will most often see them flying across the wind, and occasionally downwind, you will just about never see them battling their way into it. This is the genius of the process of natural selection that has brought them to this point, and why distance, far from being their enemy, is their home.

The individual bird that I was watching was travelling across the sea by exploiting the differential between the low air pressure just above the waves and the higher pressure a foot or so above. In the two phases of its flight, it was first achieving progress towards its desired direction by a short, fixed-wing glide within inches of the water where the air resistance is lowest; then, when its progress slowed, it rose up above the waves, turned half downwind and flapped its straight wings three or four times in order to achieve sufficient height and speed from which to turn, descend and glide again. While in the 'power gathering' phase, it would turn over on its side the better to expose the full underside of its wings to the wind, which explains how someone watching will alternately see the black of its back (during the glide) and the white of its underside. As another appreciative observer put it: 'They fly a foot or two above the water as if attached and moulded to it.'*

As I watched them, it struck me forcefully that I didn't want to just park my enthusiasm when the ferry docked in Mallaig, to start again only when I next happened to come this way. Sure, I could learn all there was to learn from books, videos and academic papers, but I would know the shearwaters no better if I did. Against the backdrop of the Skye Cuillins and the Sound of Sleat, I started to articulate a foolish promise to myself. The promise was that I would follow these birds wherever they took me for the coming year, for one cycle of their lives. In that time, I would learn all I could, and allow myself to be changed, or not, by whatever I learned.

....

* *The Seabird's Cry*, Adam Nicolson (William Collins, 2017).

It was a strange and impractical resolution for a man with no particular head for heights, and who got seasick watching pirate films.

⟶⟨⟶

Caroline was standing against the railing with her sketch book, pencilling in the shapes and scales of the receding islands as an *aide memoire* to some future painting.

'You're quiet,' she said. It was a simple observation that allowed me either to confront, dodge or ignore it. Besides, it was a rare enough event for her not to allow it to pass unappreciated.

I had spent the last few months researching for a book on the crisis within the insect biomass, and, by degrees, I was finding myself distanced from it. This was partly because the science and observation required was of an order higher than I seemed to possess, but also because there was a depressing one-way inevitability about it all, which was getting to me. It wasn't so much the worryingly clean car windscreens or the house windows that were no longer plastered by tiger moths, or the butterflies and solitary bees we no longer saw around the garden. It was more that you could follow this lack all the way up through the food chain to insect feeders like spotted flycatchers and cuckoos and beyond, and begin to understand that our species has simply become the unwitting architect of an invisible and largely silent Armageddon. Nowhere was this made clearer than in a piece of German research[4] showing that, over a 27-year period from 1989 the annual average total weight of flying insects – their biomass – in the study area had declined by 76%. That is a fall of three quarters in the number of pollinators at the bottom end of the food chain, and I increasingly felt that it needed someone with more authority on the subject than me to shout about it. It didn't help that the same people who would run marathons for elephant sanctuaries, and chain themselves to railings to help save the rhino, appeared not to be moved by the plight of insects.

'Good thing, too,' one of my friends had said at a recent picnic when I had mentioned the 76% statistic. 'Keeps them out of my food.'

Also, I happened to be at a time of my life when I wanted to tell positive stories, not sad ones.

'I was just thinking,' I said to Caroline. I often said this, and normally it meant that I wasn't thinking at all, or, if I was, it was about county cricket scores, which bored her.

'And?'

'About insects, if you must know.' I smiled at her, as she knew all too well of my creative struggles, and we had talked about it a good deal on our holiday.

'And what were you thinking?'

'That I'd rather think about that lot.' I waved an arm at the ceaseless traffic of seabirds around us.

It wasn't that easy, of course, just chucking out five months of effort, or at least putting it on the back-burner, but one of the gifts of ageing is the long-sightedness that allows you to spot a dead end before you actually reach it. The fact of the insects being so much more important to the future of mankind than the shearwaters may well have been unarguable, but I could not change who I was, or what I thought. Once you knew who you were, I had found over the years, the trick was to work as closely with the grain as you practically could, always assuming it was legal, honest and decent.

'Which ones?' she asked, and then after a pause: 'You don't need to answer, by the way. I know.'

For a while, we just watched the Hebridean islands receding into the noonday haze, and contented ourselves with drinking in the unmanning beauty of it all.

'What's wrong with that?' she said, without waiting for my answer. 'Go for it.'

4. THE OXBRIDGE SEABIRD

Early August

She was a great one for recycling, even back in the 1970s, so it was no surprise that for my sixteenth birthday my grandmother gave me her Kirkman and Jourdain's classic 1930 edition of *British Birds*. Inside it was a hand-written card telling me that this would be followed by her old binoculars at Christmas, urging me to be honest with myself in my identification claims, and to come back to Mull as often as I could.

For all its beautiful illustrations and precious inaccuracies, her choice of gift had misjudged the boy, who had temporarily moved on from birds and into his monosyllabic teenage wastelands, with posters of Bond girls and Lamborghinis on the walls of his bedroom, and a bicycle to act as a chariot for the few dreams he happened to have at the time. Deep down and in her wisdom, she probably knew that this was always going to happen, and that it would also herald a more complex phase in our friendship where the key inputs from her own side for a time would have to be a thick skin and deep reserves of patience.

'I absolutely love that beautiful bird book you gave me', I had fibbed in the thank-you letter that followed, when the truth was that all I had really wanted was a moped, or money towards one. Mopeds were an awkward 49cc metaphor for breaking out of domesticated boyhood and for the ensuing freedoms that beckoned somewhere out there beyond the A272 and the Rother Valley. Reading about birds was a thing for past years and possibly future decades, so Kirkman and Jourdain duly went straight up into my bookshelf, where they remained indignantly sandwiched between the 1971 *Beano Yearbook* and an old copy of *Jane's Fighting Planes*, for the time being no more relevant to my life than Wagner's Ring Cycle.

But always her letters came, full of Mull news, the exotic doings of the locals and of frustrated empire loyalism, painstakingly banged out on the Smith Corona. For my own part, she remained the only person with whom I felt I could be almost entirely honest about myself and my thoughts, and I kept writing to her long after correspondence had otherwise become an unwelcome chore in my life. As far as I was concerned, she was on my side, a rare commodity indeed within my confected teenage awkwardness.

A short note came in response to my thank-you letter for the Kirkman and Jourdain book, thanking me for mine, and telling me that Sandy the arthritic retriever had finally gone to her 'happy hunting ground' the afternoon before. 'I have cried too much,' she ended, both admitting to and openly defying her own vulnerability.

I held the letter and tried for a long moment to avoid thinking of her crying. Without ever consciously articulating the thought, it was perhaps the first time I properly understood that I might one day cry for her too, as we eventually do for everyone.

———◦———

If birds were literary devices, the Manx shearwater might stand for irony.

The name itself implies that there should be a thriving population on the Isle of Man, whereas the truth is that there are none.* They went away many years ago, courtesy of the brown rat. The Latin name, *Puffinus puffinus*, also cleverly disguises the fact that they are entirely unrelated to the puffin (*Fratercula arctica*), repeating the wordplay in case anyone didn't get it first time round. In fact, purists would say that the correct name of the northern version of the Manx shearwater is *Puffinus puffinus puffinus*, a classifier's 'So there!' if ever there was one. And, counterintuitively, the best way of finding an adult shearwater on a summer's day is to walk in diametrically the opposite direction from its home. Because, wherever else it will be, it will not be there.

....

* There are a few on the Calf of Man, a small adjacent island that the rats haven't (yet) colonised.

The pace of irony quickens when considering its behaviour. Evolution prescribed that Manxies, to avoid predation, should come in to land only on the darkest of nights, but then also saw to it that they would be almost entirely unequipped to do so, flying virtually blind and regularly crashing into fences, farm buildings and even people.* Most seabirds fly straight into, or close to, their nest, while the Manxie, whose feet are set too far back for anything other than an awkward, shuffling movement, tends to land far enough away from its burrow to give a sporting chance to any marauding black-backed gull that happens to be up late and on the lookout for a meal.

But the biggest irony of all is to be found on their breeding grounds, where they are inactive for all but the darkest few hours of the night. Take Skomer Island off the Welsh coast, home to the world's largest colony. With 350,000 breeding pairs, there are likely to be in excess of a million birds in, on and around the little island during the peak breeding season and yet a visitor there on, say, a late July day will not see one of them. Not one. Delighted by the photogenic puffins, they probably won't mind and perhaps won't even know that under their feet is massed a honeycomb world of a third of a million burrows, each of which contains one embryonic master mariner waiting for a parent to return at night from its foraging expedition, alert for the strengthening signal deep within that will soon draw it outwards into the infinity of wind and

....

* The team working on shearwaters from their hut on Skomer Island regard the regular night-time thumps, falls and bruises they incur from unguided, speeding birds as no more than an occupational hazard.

waves beyond the southern horizon. With the island's area of 700 acres, that is around 500 burrows per football pitch area of land, or not far off one for every square metre. Put another way, 450 tons of a largely invisible bird lives there.

But, as the scientific community has found for 70 years or more, a bird that spends most of its life down a hole or out on the oceans gives up its secrets reluctantly.

The Manx shearwater has come a long way to be here, and a quick glance at how it has done this might help to sneak us past the border guards of the bird's modern life.

From quadruped dinosaur 240 million years ago to ocean wanderer today, the radiating evolution of seabirds shines a powerful spotlight into how birds in general, and shearwaters in particular, developed. Although no one fully knows all the answers, there seems little doubt that quadruped became biped for agility, front limbs became wings for flexibility, and short wings became longer wings for distance. Later on, feathers gradually became longer, digits fused at the end of wings, and wishbones developed to allow wings to develop their own forward thrust; bones duly became thinner and lighter, and the bony tail shortened in line with the evolution of a keel-like breastbone that gave essential stability in flight. At this point, maybe 120 million years ago and with all the jumping and gliding from hills and trees behind them, they had passed beyond the rudimentary archaeopteryx and become true birds.

Then, while most birds stayed broadly on land, a small percentage evolved to take advantage of the vast empty spaces and rich marine diet available out in the oceans. To equip themselves for this life, they developed longer wings for a life at sea, webbed feet for power on and in the water, salt glands to process the by-product of a marine diet, and a sense of smell to lead them to food and to bring them home. Their plumage became denser for waterproofing and insulation and, unlike land birds, they generally stuck to a mix of just three colours – black, white and grey – so as better to conceal themselves from both their predators and their prey. In many cases, the tips of their wings would be black, the melanin giving extra strength and so reducing wear. By and large, they developed a habit of loyalty to the same breeding ground, of crowding together in those grounds for protection, and of laying just one egg each season, because that is what nature had taught them gave the best chance of long-term success.*

Down through the evolutionary eras they cascaded, until eventually they split into the six basic forms of seabird we have around us today: penguins, petrels, pelicans, gulls, divers and tropicbirds. Out into the different ecosystems they flew: some to brackish coastal marshes, some to the highest and least accessible cliffs and some, like the petrels, to their remote ocean wildernesses. The petrels then split into four smaller family groups: albatrosses, petrels, storm petrels and shearwaters.

....

* Compare with the new-born stonechat clutch, for example, whose mother stops feeding them after about twenty days, and whose father chases them off the territory afterwards, so that a new nest can be built and the next of maybe three broods embarked on.

Generally these became the great oceanic travellers, coming to land simply and solely to breed, often in burrows, and otherwise staying well out to sea, often covering vast distances between breeding seasons, or just for foraging. And we know the rest: the shearwaters split into somewhere between nineteen and 25 sub-species, depending on where you draw the line, one of which, the Manx, settled on a few small patches of land off the western reaches of the north European island group for its breeding grounds, and where it remains, one of 11,000 species of bird alive in the world today. You only have to go back fourteen stops on the phylogenetic tree of life to connect the shearwater directly with the ostrich at one end, and the bee-eater at the other, every single one descending from something that looked much like an archaeopteryx.

Creatures evolve to pass the best possible genes to future generations, and the Manxie won't stop here; already, it has given rise to two almost identical evolutionary branches (the Balearic and the yelkouan, who operate at opposite ends of the Mediterranean), and inevitable geographical separation within those species will in turn give birth to more, because evolution is an unstoppable process, not a finite event.

One of the evolutionary drivers in the next century or so will inevitably be climate change and, specifically, the warming oceans. As with most European species, the breeding grounds will tend to drift northwards, to become less extensive and lead to smaller populations than before, to extinctions even.[1] There will be other drivers – availability of fish stocks, concentrations of micro-plastics, predator control – all of which will aggregate in a slow Darwinian plod towards the best genetic changes needed for survival. One lesson from this story was that I was only observing the shearwater in a single moment in time, no more than the blink of an eye in the whole length of its natural history.

One year I would be following them for. Just one year in the sweeping arc of 125 million.

So I had to start somewhere.

⌇

Explaining why birds became my passion might help.

Numbers, that's why. I have lived a life almost comically defined by numbers and lists, so it's hardly surprising that the passion for birds grew ever deeper within me once I had allowed them back into my life in my twenties.

For me as a younger man, birds were flying numbers made manifestly beautiful, statistics in a thousand different plumages. Depending on who you listen to, there are 11,122 bird species in the world today,[2] which would be 164 more were it not for the extinctions of the last five centuries. Each of these vanished species, the last three of which in 2020 were the cryptic treehunter and the Alagoas foliage-gleaner from Brazil and the po'ouli from Hawaii, is a little ecosystemic tragedy in its own right. 574 species have been recorded at least once in Britain,[3] from the ubiquitous wren to the once-seen long-billed murrelet, around 250 species going so far as to breed here. If you are interested, and you would genuinely be the first person on earth to have felt this way, my life list runs to 1,202 species, of which the Manx shearwater was 83, as we have seen, and the wandering albatross 193. An auditor would probably knock 50 or so off that total with justification, to take into account a rather cavalier attitude to accuracy in my late twenties, when a bullfinch could easily be a black-headed gonolek if it, and I, tried hard enough.

Birdwatching lends itself to list-building, both as a record of experience and as an end in itself. At its most innocent it might be the joy of a straightforward sighting of, say, the giant kingfisher (bird 1,003), and at its most devious it is trying to contort the very standard bird you are looking at through your binoculars on a Scottish beach into the similar, but much rarer one that you would dearly like it to be. Taken to extremes to which I am glad to say I never quite descended, it morphs into mad night-time dashes across the country to follow up on reports of a rare vagrant in some supermarket car park in Cornwall, and even beyond that to skulduggery, with the aim of stopping anyone else seeing 'your' bird. Friends and family commented frequently on the triviality of measuring out my birdwatching in lists without ever understanding that its triviality was precisely why I was doing it. Things that, on the surface, don't really matter so often become the very things that bring uncomplicated delight. It's the things that matter that are generally the problem.

Over the years, though, my priorities have changed. Adding to the life list has grown progressively less important in direct contrast to wanting to find out more about whichever bird I was looking at, and the wider ecosystem it inhabited. Everything, as Leonardo da Vinci pointed out,* is connected to

---

* Or Lenin. Or Sir Humphrey Appleby.

everything else, and natural history becomes a whole lot more compelling when you untangle the co-evolutionary relation-ships between the things that interest you. Also, the older I got, the more conscious I became of the fragility of the lives of the birds with whom we share our bruised planet. Gradually, the field guides that lined my bookshelves in my twenties gave way to books about conservation, personal natural history accounts, and the literature of birds. I felt that only by knowing more could I explain more, and by explaining more, I could perhaps persuade people around me to care about what we have, and what we might lose. In spending many hundreds of hours unwit-tingly disturbing birds and invading their private moments, I could at least use what I learned to be an advocate for them as I got older.

From my rainy railway carriage window on the way home from our trip to Rum, I watched a curlew beat its way into the wind, the headwaters of the Upper Clyde flowing darkly north between the forestry blocks at Elvanfoot. I understood more clearly with every southward mile the power of the gift I had regained from my childhood that weekend. I would soon be back again. Yesterday's resolution hadn't just been a pipe dream.

After all, this was a journey that I had spent half my life making – until my 27th year, when I suddenly stopped coming.

By the time we arrived home later that night, two truths had slowly wreathed themselves into my embryonic planning process.

The first was that the birds to which I had just dedicated the next year of my life were inconveniently going to be 8,000 miles away within a couple of months and until half the year was done, shearing the ocean waves over a warm southern sea. That, after all, is what a Manx shearwater is best known for: the 20,000-mile round and clockwise journey that it makes each year from its British breeding grounds,[4] down past Africa, across to Argentina and then back up via the Caribbean to north-western Europe again. The second truth was even simpler: hitherto, birds had always just been an innocent pleasure in my life, and certainly not a subject for detailed academic research.

'Roger wears what little scholarship he has with elegance', said some witty science teacher years ago, in an end-of-term school report laced with cruel accuracy. 'He has an enviable knack of creating strong opinions out of a fact vacuum.'

But I had to start somewhere. The shearwaters I had seen on Rum the previous week would shortly begin the long trek down to their southern summer and would be further and further away from me with each sporadic beat of their wings. If I went back to their breeding grounds in a few weeks, all I would find would be empty burrows and the wheeling and screaming of the resident herring gulls and skuas far below. I, on the other hand, was sitting at my desk late at night, looking at an unhelpful computer screen into whose principal search engine I had optimistically typed the words 'Manx shearwater'. Thrilled to be under way, I fixated for a while on the first concrete fact I came upon, which was that the birds' average weight was somewhere between 400 and 450 grams. Initially, I couldn't visualise what 400 grams felt like, so I collected the kitchen scales and wandered around the house picking up random objects until one of them, a 400-page paperback book, came to the same number. Expressed another way, this meant that something not much larger, and certainly no heavier, than a dog-eared schoolboy copy of Evelyn Waugh's *Sword of Honour* trilogy would fly around four million miles in its life, and not touch land for maybe a thousand days after launching its infant self westwards into the vast and stormy spaces of its first flight. It was with that odd comparison that my adventure truly took to wings of its own.

By the following weekend, I had the beginnings of a plan. I had simply and politely asked the search engine who were the world experts on the Manx shearwater and thus, serendipitously, I found out that the majority of them lived in the British Isles. Logical, really, when that is where their study birds breed. 'Dr M. Brooke', it told me, and 'Professor T. Guilford'.

A few weeks later, I found myself walking in from Cambridge railway station to see one of them, Dr Mike Brooke at the Zoology Department, to start the process in earnest. As the family's sole, self-conscious non-graduate, that walk felt good, as if my invitation to go and question one of the world's leading seabird experts in one of its great universities somehow conferred honorary academic status on me, lifting me above the queues of tourists snaking their curious way around the city. I ordered my sandwich from the deli counter in the vague, pre-occupied way that I imagined an academic might do if his head were full of formulae, or shearwater feathers. At the University

Museum of Zoology, where I received my first sharp lesson in making appointments if I wanted to see the non-public exhibits, I told the receptionist that I was researching a book on seabirds, as if this priceless fact in itself would quickly unlock doors that had been previously slammed shut in my face.

'Everyone here is writing a book,' she said, without looking up. 'That's what they all do in Cambridge.' If I wanted to see the shallow drawers full of shearwaters and their eggs, I would have to come back once I had submitted my requests in triplicate, and achieved some academic backing.

Initially, what I found from Mike Brooke was what I had already guessed I would find: that the essence of the Manx shearwater is distance. Distance and navigation.

From DPhil to warden to scientist to curator, Mike's professional trajectory has always been in pursuit of seabirds and, most particularly, the Manx shearwater, and it would be hard to find someone who has dedicated more of their life to them, or contributed more to our understanding of them.

From fish to reptile, to bird, to seabird, to shearwater, to Manx shearwater, the bird's evolutionary trajectory has always been seawards and skywards, perhaps distancing itself from the apex predator-in-chief, man. When, later in my searches, I asked Professor Chris Perrins, who has worked with these birds since the early 1960s, where he thought the next stage of their development lay, he paused for a while and then said: 'They'll probably stay as they are and just divide into a couple more subdivisions.' A year later, I came to see his point: they are already supremely adapted to the way they live, and the environment in which they spend their time.

Few of those millions of miles that a shearwater will fly in its life will be accidental ones, and science from the last 70 years has slowly been unpicking what 'maps' the bird reads, and how, what paths it follows, under what impulses and to which deadlines. During that time, we have progressed from knowing only that this bird is migratory to understanding not only where it goes, but what routes it takes, how long it flies for, or forages for, how deep it dives and for which fish, how and when it sleeps and how much of magnetism, smell, memory and instinct it deploys to take it to where it needs to be. The only major thing we still don't truly understand is where it goes in its first couple of summers; we are starting to get there, but the miracle of scientific research is that each answer really just poses the next set of questions. What we do know is that when that 70-day-old fledgling launches itself off its windswept hilltop for the very first time, it does so without its parents' guidance and it will not touch land again for at least the next two years, very possibly four.

Scientific discovery tends to progress in steps and jumps rather than straight lines, and there was a pivotal such day in July 1953. It was from the Cambridge University Library roof, no more than 600 yards from the Zoology Department office where I found myself sitting with Mike Brooke, that a small number of shearwaters were released on that day, in a celebrated experiment that moved the infant science of bird navigation a great leap forward. For the previous twenty years, a Welsh ornithologist called Ronald Lockley* had been arranging for visitors to his island home at Skokholm to take away with them a few breeding shearwaters to see how long it took them to get back from the places they were released – Dartington, Frensham, Venice and Boston, among others. Most of those that survived the outward journeys eventually made it back, but in varying timescales that left open the question of whether they had done so by a sea or land route, and therefore of what characteristics they would have needed to make whatever journey they did. The next giant name in the development of the science of bird navigation, a Cambridge academic called Geoffrey Matthews, started to collaborate with Lockley at this point, and it is perhaps the latter's work in his home city that produces the defining step change in our understanding of how they find their way from one point to another.†

That night in 1953, four of the twenty birds that had been released from Cambridge under cloudy skies earlier in the day were back in their burrows off the west coast of Wales, a distance of 240 miles, having had to achieve average ground

....

* A name that is forever linked to the Manx shearwater, through the passionate research and writing he did on their behalf, just as Joy Adamson is inextricably linked to lions, and Gavin Maxwell to otters.

† A delightful story from this era involved John Barrett (warden of Dale Fort field centre on the Welsh mainland opposite Skokholm) who found that the Great Western Railway would happily carry pigeons on Skokholm's behalf ('acceptable livestock') but not shearwaters ('unacceptable livestock') for their research journeys up to Cambridge. Barrett, himself a no-nonsense veteran of Stalag Luft III prison camp in 1943, got around the problem by simply labelling his shearwaters as 'donkeys', which made them entirely acceptable to GWR.

speeds of around 30 miles per hour to do so even by the most direct route, meaning overland. Birds need two abilities for navigation: a sense of orientation to give them direction, and a mind map to give them a start point; so, to have achieved what they did, the Cambridge birds had unarguably flown across completely unknown land (not their usual element of sea), done so without any possibly familiar waymarks, and proved more or less conclusively for the first time that wild birds had an innate navigational ability.* Science would later work out what attributes they used to do this, but there was no doubting that they had successfully orientated themselves in the swirling, tobacco-scented skies above undergraduate 1950s Cambridge, established which was the right direction home, and then flown directly there until they found visual landmarks that eventually led them to their burrows.

The shearwater belongs to the order Procellariiformes, sharing it with albatrosses, petrels and the tiny storm petrels. These are the 'storm birds', landing only to breed, long-lived, industrious parents to single chicks and, up to a point, faithful partners. They are the 'edge-choosers, creatures whose lives have stepped beyond the ordinary into environments of such difficulty that they can respond only with a slow, cumulative mastery which

....

* *The Manx Shearwater*, Michael Brooke (T. & A.D. Poyser, 1990). The very readable academic masterpiece which any enthusiast needs to hand, and to which this book owes much.

amounts in the end to genius'.* They vary in size from the smallest of all seabirds (the least storm petrel, who weighs in at about 30 grams) to the largest of the lot, the wandering albatross, whose wingspan is twelve times that of its distant cousin and whose weight is greater by a factor of nearly 300.† One identifying feature common across the whole order is its tube nose, what look like nostrils high up on its beak, a vital part of its navigational system.

Relatively quickly, I came to love the science and scientific research involved in learning about the shearwater, at the same intensity with which I had loathed it at school. Science, I discovered, enabled things to be never entirely right or entirely wrong, and therefore for every extreme view I held to be theoretically plausible. For me, those Cambridge shearwaters proved beyond any doubt that birds had their own internal navigational systems, whereas the truly academic brain was enchained by the 'whys' and 'wherefores' of the other birds that hadn't made it back so quickly. 'Proves nothing,' said Professor Tim Guilford of the Oxford Zoology Department with a faint smile, when I asked him, 'other than a strong probability.' The uncertainty was refreshing, life-enhancing even, and many times during the coming months I would meet head-on Karl Popper's falsification premise by which, in science, things can only be proved false, or likely, but never true. For someone who had spent a

....

* *The Seabird's Cry*, Adam Nicolson.
† The two birds are displayed, stuffed, in comical juxtaposition in the same cabinet at Oxford's Museum of Natural History. The albatross looks a bit moth-eaten, while the petrel has an air of lingering disappointment, envy even.

lifetime cheerfully accepting the existence of gravity just by thinking about apples, it was a rude awakening.

Incrementally, I created an 'idiot's guide' to the Manx shearwater on the wall above my desk, alongside an old French print of the bird itself:

1. Lives for up to 50 years.
2. Marries for life.
3. Only lays one egg in any season.
4. Rears chick in a burrow, either dug by itself or a rabbit.
5. Commutes 20,000 clockwise miles round the Atlantic each year with the trade winds. Spends the northern winter over a southern ocean.
6. Eats small fish, squid, molluscs and plankton. Shallow diver. Each feeding trip might be 2,000 miles or more.
7. Flies across the wind by 'shearing' the edges of waves with dynamic soaring.
8. Feet set well back, so not a good mover on land, other than climbing small cliffs, which it does with the help of its beak.
9. 80% of the world's population breed on west coast of UK, most on Skomer and Skokholm Islands off south-west Wales, and Rum.
10. Sits with others on the water, often in huge rafts, when not flying, particularly in the early evening while waiting for dark.
11. Flies in to its breeding burrow only when dark, and preferably raining and a bit windy.
12. Weird night call that sounds like a cross between a roosting pheasant and a child crying.

An expert is someone who knows more and more about less and less; and, like a well-set treasure hunt, my initial researches not only gave me priceless information but also referred me ever onwards in the direction of other experts, all of whom gave freely of their time. That, I found, was the defining quality of natural historians: their willingness to pass their passion and expertise on to those who asked for it, and needed it.

Bit by bit, article by article, book by book, I thrust myself deeper into the wilderness world of the Manx shearwater, collecting flecks of information like a lint roller on an old suit. It was all rather like being sixteen again, only without the Deep Purple LPs, the acne and the underlying anger.

If I had achieved nothing else, I had re-learned how to learn.

There is some argument over whether the parents actually hang around for a little in the vicinity once they have stopped feeding their chick (they probably do) but there is no doubting that the shearwater chick is on its own in the question of deciding the right moment to go, and which direction to fly once the wind first blows into the underside of its wings. From that point on, from that moment when the chick comes awkwardly out of the burrow on some moonless night, a powerful instinct imprinted within its brain will draw it ever southwards, and then westwards, to its southern summer. The parents will have no more part in that journey than mine did in my army career. Actually less, because at least my parents sent me the odd letter.

Thinking about those chicks, I started to plan to spend what was left of the breeding season getting up as close and personal as I could with them. This isn't as easy as it sounds, mainly because what suits a shearwater by way of a breeding site is in inverse proportion to its accessibility for humans. Then, out of the blue, I received an email from Tim Guilford with some old but useful academic papers attached, and an apology that he would be out of touch for around a month, as he would be on St Kilda, and then Rum, supervising some field research projects.

'Do you want a hand?' I replied, purely speculatively, in the way that I might have asked for an unlikely upgrade at the check-in before a long and uncomfortable flight.

'Come along,' he said. 'Probably easier to come to Rum at this stage, and not St Kilda.'

'You'll need a tent,' he added. 'The hut only just fits two of us in.' Having spent nine years being paid by the British tax-payer to carry tents around in their service, and then sleep in them, I rather thought to have seen the last of them, other than the very comfortable ones with fridges in the side compartment.

Thus I found myself heading back the 600 or so miles to Mallaig a few short weeks after I had left it.

I was starting my adventure in earnest.

5. AN ISLAND FULL OF NOISES

Isle of Rum

....

Any time I feel lost, I pull out a map and stare.
I stare until I have reminded myself that life is
a giant adventure, so much to do, to see.
ANGELINA JOLIE

....

I have an old and faded Kodak print of my grandmother sitting on a cairn at the summit of Mull's highest mountain, Ben More, in the summer of 1976. She is wearing faded red jeans that are slightly too short for her, and an old blue denim shirt. Her hair is blowing around wildly as she faces westwards into the prevailing wind, and she is feeding biscuits to her dog. It is a remarkable feature of my remaining photographs of her just how often she is feeding biscuits to her dog.

Looking back at it, I suspect that it was one of her last trips up that mountain before she had to leave it to others younger and stronger than herself. Although not by any means a difficult climb, it is a long and relentless pull up from the little promontory on the edge of Loch na Keal, and it catches out those who do not look after themselves, a category in which the ashtrays full of unfiltered Turkish cigarettes on her kitchen table suggested that she belonged. But hill climbing, as she saw it, was a back door into adventure which, itself, was a gateway to virtue, and it all marked out our stays on the island as part boot camp, part life behind the bike sheds. Our annual trip up Ben More, as Mull's only Munro, was a ritual, normally on the last full day I was there. Just about the only way that anyone could get off joining her was X-ray proof of a broken bone or a well-crafted excuse about having to do some highly implausible schoolwork. She didn't act a very convincing sweet old lady but, then again, you might also think that most teenage boys would rather have a gang leader.

Ben More is a dominant presence from just about any part of Mull and its surrounding seas, and over the years it became something of a lodestone for me, more significant than just a 966-metre pyramid of igneous rocks. Climbing it was something I found I could do that others didn't seem able to, not necessarily because they physically couldn't, but because they didn't actually want to. Academically middle of the road and a sporting disaster area, I was content to mark off my achievements alone, or in company, each time I reached the top and put my next rock on the summit cairn, each one strengthening my resolve a little more. I turned out to be quite good at putting one foot in front of the other and walking up steep hills, to the extent that, in my twenties, I made something of a career of it.

Sometimes, if I was on my own, I would sit up there and write nature poetry of such grim pointlessness that even I knew it belonged only in the bin into which, after an encouraging comment or two, my grandmother would normally quietly consign it later on in the evening. My excuse for writing poems was that I was studying Wordsworth and the Romantic poets for my A-levels; her excuse for chucking them away was that they were truly awful.

Whether by accident or design, though, she had cunningly used Ben More as a metaphor for achievement for a teenager who had rather few of them in his locker. Get him to realise how good reaching the summit of anything is, was the way her thinking might have gone, and you will eventually get him finding his own summits, and then climbing them. To a surprising extent, my relationship with the mountain she gifted me defined who I would become, good or bad, and over the years I climbed it about 30 times.

Equally and rather sadly, she did not do relaxation. Just as she could not walk into a room and not see things that needed to be done to it, so she could never walk round her garden and not see the weeds. The devil made work for idle hands, as far as she was concerned, and it was her job to unlearn us of all the bad routines of school and a life living around busy parents. The more I got to know her, the more she inculcated in me that notion of Kipling's about filling the unforgiving minute with sixty seconds' worth of distance run. Over the years, it was often all I needed to get out of myself and try something new, but it also left me with half a lifetime's ignorance of the joys of living in the moment.

Ambition and restlessness, those were her gifts, a list to which you might also reasonably add Turkish cigarettes, unsuitable music hall songs and the benefit of some very bizarre political opinions.

It was a shearwater restlessness, though, one that was fated consistently to seek out what lay beyond the harbour bar.

〜

It was some of that restlessness that now took me back up to Rum, but it felt right enough to be on the road so soon. A modern life can easily become full of artificial timetables and deadlines, so it was good to have no more concrete a plan than just to meet someone, somewhere, sometime, on a mountain 600 miles to the north; and to have no sense of how to get there more detailed than to arrive in Mallaig and get on a boat. The prospect of travelling alone without a timetable is an exciting one, particularly when it doesn't involve the desolate loneliness of an airport departure lounge and the isolation of a city hotel. In my experience, travelling on my own has seldom been lonely; it was travelling in cities with millions of people that was always the problem.

There is little academic agreement as to whether seabirds get lonely but, if they do, there is plenty of opportunity for it. Appearing to socialise for the purposes of protection rather than company, shearwaters will spend around 90% of their lives alone, only coming together for breeding, rafting and for the occasional rich food source, like a mid-ocean trawler. But it's in the last few weeks before they fledge that the sense of being utterly alone must be at its strongest. Twenty hours a day is the least amount of time that they will spend alone, and even those four hours of parental company will vanish for good soon enough.

By mid-August, the shearwater chick has generally exceeded its parents' weight, and is processing as much food as they can carry up to the burrow. Keeping it fed is an all-consuming occupation for them.

Those adult shearwaters I had seen south of Rum a few weeks before would have been heading off for, or returning from, foraging runs that could go out as far as the fisheries way off to the west of Ireland, using maps laid down in their minds over many years. The nights are gradually lengthening again on those northern isles, but they still have only a short window, around four hours, when instinct tells them they are safe to return to the burrow. The other twenty hours are taken up in travelling out to their feeding grounds, fishing and then rafting up waiting for the safety of complete darkness.

The chick itself knows instinctively not to venture out to the mouth of the burrow, let alone beyond it. The compromises that evolution made to create the supreme flier also left it largely defenceless on the ground, and its wings and feathers are not yet developed enough to allow for escape by flight. With only a slightly hooked beak for fighting its own corner, it would be unlikely to survive any lengthy daytime trip outside to inspect its surroundings.

But nature's breeding seasons are so often a race against time and, for the shearwater, it is a frighteningly simple one. In a few days' time, some unseen signal will start to call the

75,000 or so adults on the Rum colonies inexorably southwards and away from the burrows, after which the chicks must
rely on little more than extreme hunger and the growing need
to, quite literally, spread their wings.

High up on the sides of Hallival, in the very colony I had
incompetently stumbled on a few weeks before, Tim Guilford
and his PhD student, Ollie Padget, would be using those last
days to remove and replace old geolocators* off the leg rings of
the returning adults, so that the mystery of their huge journeys
could be better known, and simultaneously applying them to
the unfledged chicks, to start to get a better understanding of
where they actually go for their first two southern summers.

Just about everything in bird science comes down to the
tiny increments of routine observation and experiment that,
aggregated, may or may not lead to a measurable advance
in knowledge. This is not a world of sudden flashes of light in
laboratories so much as one of woolly hats and grubby finger-
nails. If there are 'eureka' moments, then they arrive over long
periods of time, and after an awful lot of tea.

I wandered out of Kinloch, Rum's sole settlement, and up the
Dibidil path southwards in the direction of the high ground of
Hallival to find Tim and Ollie.

....

* A geolocator is a simple, small and light tracking device, comprising
battery, light sensor, clock and memory chip. They record light levels
which, when measured against day length, can be used to estimate latitude (British Trust for Ornithology).

'You'll find us at grid reference 397971,' Tim had texted. 'Give us a shout if you get stuck.'

It didn't matter that there was no phone reception anyway – hell would have to freeze over for an ex-soldier in his late fifties to admit that he couldn't find his way to an exact grid reference, especially one at the top end of a large bog and below a cliff face on an island entirely devoid of landmarks. Pride simply would not have allowed it. The evening before I left home, having checked the old tent that our boys had used for their Duke of Edinburgh expeditions and found it full of rot, I had hurriedly borrowed one from a local friend that now seemed to weigh around the same as the Albert Hall. Ethics may very well dictate that only 3% extra weight can be added to birds in the scientific equipment that they carry, but in my own case it was around 40%, and I wandered up the long, rocky path looking like an inelegant, slow-moving Christmas tree.

After a couple of false crests, concealed bogs and misleading valleys, I found the little research hut they were working from, broke out the camping gas stove and made a pasta supper to share with my Oxford friends. Not for the last time, making a meal for people who were doing me a favour was the only currency in which I could pay the scientific community into whose work I was lumbering.

On Hallival, Tim told me about the geolocators we would be collecting from the returning shearwaters. They needed to know more about the exact journeys the various birds made once they flew from Rum: where they went, how long they stayed there, and how directly they travelled. Frustratingly, a geolocator only reveals its secrets to the researcher once it has been removed from the leg of a returning bird a year or two years after it has been fixed; its great advantage, however, is that the battery lasts for a couple of years and a vast amount of travel information spills out once it is plugged into a base computer. That information, when plotted on a chart and aggregated with the data from a couple of dozen other birds from the same colony, starts to build up a detailed picture of where they have been, both on their migrations and also on their breeding-related foraging trips. With built-in salt water immersion loggers, the picture is complemented by an idea of how long the birds have spent on or in the sea. But like so much shearwater science, the exercise could only be carried out when everyone else was safely tucked up in their beds.

After dark, we scrambled up another 300 or 400 feet to a steep section of the Hallival colony that the Oxnav* researchers used for their studies. It was similar to the one that I had stumbled on a few weeks earlier, except this one had a series of painted pebbles that marked out the 40 or so 'study' burrows from which the research information was gathered. Far down below us was the sea, the gulls and the huge unseen rafts of adult shearwaters; up above and around us on the side of the escarpment were the burrows and their hungry occupants. In between, two scientists and a writer, waiting for the show to begin. For a minute or two, with a view of the sunset on the skerries and silent tidal rips of what seemed to be the entire Hebridean archipelago, it felt like everything I had been born

....

* Based at Oxford University, Oxnav research focuses on behavioural and ecological aspects of animal navigation and spatial cognition.

for was laid out in front of me for my pleasure. The blue outline of the ridge of the Skye Cuillins gradually faded into black to our north, and far below we could hear the last of the evening gulls and the call of the foraging waders somewhere out on the marshy hill.

'With this as your working life,' I asked Tim as we stared out into the fading day and waited for the arrival of the first shearwaters, 'what do you do for holidays?'

He thought about it for a bit. 'Oh, roughly the same,' he said, 'only probably in the Mediterranean, and almost certainly with a kayak.'

Ollie was the same. Once fieldwork was in your blood, it was a hard habit to break. This may have all been work towards a scientific paper and an advancement of the science of seabird navigation, but that didn't stop it being what they both loved doing, something I found with just about all the scientists I was to come across.

Night fell on Ardnamurchan, to our south. We watched the pinprick lights of the crofts and cottages of Sanna and Portuairk and then the low orange glow of Mallaig opposite. There was a dizzying lack of solidity in the steep bank we were on, looking out at the view like theatre-goers up in the gods; it all gave me a sense of slowly tipping forward into the view. Tiredness, brought about by the late hour and a long day, made that sense of tipping something of an inevitability.

'Those Mallaig lights,' said Tim, after a while. 'They provide a unique challenge for the fledgling shearwaters. Quite a number mistake them for the moon, particularly on moonless nights, or for the gleam of light on the sea, and they land there in error on their maiden flight. No one quite understands why. But there's quite a lot of research being done on it.'

'What happens then? Once they've landed?' I already knew that a shearwater was ill-equipped for even the shortest journeys on land.

'Quite often they are found in gardens and streets in the morning. They can't find enough height, or wind, to take off, so they are just stuck. We call it "grounding".* They get collected, put in shoeboxes and then taken back out to sea on the ferry and "relaunched".† Of course, some aren't so fortunate. A cat or a skua would make short work of a stranded bird.'

He might have gone on to say that the really unlucky ones will 'stumble into the ganglands of Mallaig's gulls, where they are peeled and eaten as swiftly as a banana'.‡

I was fascinated by the notion of a young animal heading off for its first journey, and an 8,000-mile odyssey to Argentina at that, not even making it more than twenty miles. It was like a round-the-world sailor capsizing in the Solent, having just set sail from Southampton.

'It's really only bad in stormy years,' he added. 'In 2012, when there were a series of bad gales, around 700 birds got

---

* Calm days are the enemy of the shearwater trying to take off from water, or flat land. Like a swan taking off from a river, the process involves much flapping, and even more paddling of the feet.

† Kind locals, coordinated by Martin Carty, whom Tim Guilford described to me as 'the Pied Piper of shearwaters', keep them overnight and then release them out at sea the following day.

‡ *Love of Country: A Hebridean Journey*, Madeleine Bunting (Granta, 2016).

rescued, and goodness knows how many didn't. It's one of the little extra challenges of leaving home in the season of equinoctial gales.'

Tim stopped talking. There was an urgent fluttering and whirring in the dark, like a bird flying around a room it has got stuck in, then a light thump behind me announced the overture. I turned round, struggling to keep my balance on the steep bank, and, in the limited red glow of my head torch, caught sight of a dark grey and white shape shuffling rapidly uphill towards the mouth of a marked burrow.

Then the noises started.

It begins with one calling bird flying out of the night towards its burrow, like a soloist in a discordant concerto. There is a tiny rushing of wind, a thud in the vicinity, and then silence. Then one bird becomes two, two becomes five, five becomes 30, and 30 becomes 500 as each section of the orchestra gets going at its own particular tempo, and the whole island seems to be given over to noise: part owl, part gull, part parrot, part howling baby. The night becomes full of fast-moving sounds, adult calling to chick, chick responding to adult, all invisible save for a second or two. Ranging from a deep chuckling to the screeching hinges of a gate into bedlam, the noises pass in front of you, behind you and above your head. Added to this are the bumps of birds landing close by, and the whooshing as they fly by within feet, sometimes within inches of your face in the darkness. At times they actually make contact with your body. Both chilling and comical, the noise continually ratchets up in volume and intensity until, at about 2.30am, everything around is unthinkably loud, as if a little bit of chaos has come to make its home here. Small wonder, I thought, that these were known as the 'devil birds' for the unearthly night-time calls they brought with them, or that the Vikings in the boats below once believed the place to be full of trolls, and sailed away.

Literature is full of references to the unearthly din but, for seabird researchers, this is all merely the background sound to their workplace, much like Radio 2 in a distribution centre.

'Oh, the noise?' said Ollie, when I mentioned its intensity after a couple of hours. 'I suppose I don't really notice it any more.'

All the while, we were moving around the pitch-black 45-degree rocky slope under the inadequate light of our red-filtered head torches, checking the study burrows, as Ronald Lockley had once done, to see whether the matchsticks in the entrance had been knocked over, and thus the parent returned. Using the inspection hatches that had been created during the previous season, we then gently took each of the study chicks and adults out, weighed and ringed them, and put them back in again with the minimum of delay and fuss. The shearwater's habit of returning to the same burrow year after year meant that, so long as the bird had survived the last twelve or 24 months, it was possible to predict with near certainty exactly where and when the ring, with all its digital information, could be retrieved.

I'm not quite sure that any part of me was designed for this process. Ollie's voice would come out of the darkness amid the mayhem announcing that '74 is back', and then Tim and I would grab the bag of tools and run over the uneven, rocky incline towards wherever the faint beam of Ollie's torch was coming from, with all of Scotland apparently vertically below us. Lurching across the rocks, and with me falling over frequently, we'd arrive, put the bird into a black felt bag, weigh it and then take it back to the lean-to to attach, or unattach, a ring with a geolocator. With all the spatial awareness and manual dexterity of a hippopotamus, my job was simply to record the weights and measures in a little pad that I couldn't see, let alone read. I was left with the notion that some bizarre readings, outliers in a twenty-year research programme, will be knocking around for the work of 2019. Then, as soon as 74 was safely back in its burrow, Ollie's disconnected voice would call once again from the blackness: 'Over here! I think I've got 29.'

In a scientific sense, those were nights when we were laying the path for research that probably wouldn't be accessible for another two years, lifting a veil from the mystery of the extraordinary journeys that these birds made; in an elemental sense, though, it felt to me like we were spectators in one of the natural world's most eerie phenomena, and it was a privilege, albeit an uncomfortable one, even to have a walk-on part.

All the same, it was only about food.

For now, *everything* is about food.

The natural world around us is criss-crossed, at any given time, with the billions and billions of intersecting lines of the animal kingdom going about the business of feeding itself. Just the domesticated honeybees in Great Britain account for around 350 billion of these flights each day, and they are but one species of British insect in a class of 27,000,[1] and one organism in our 70,000 species of living organisms[2] that needs to sustain itself on an outside source of nutrition. Together, this contributes to an unthinkably huge network of journeys that shape how we live and what we see around us. It includes the squirrel at your bird table, the fox trotting down your street at two in the morning, and even the trip you yourself will make to the supermarket this coming weekend. It is also the main reason why we see the wildlife around us: probably in excess of 90% of the animal kingdom's movements are to do with food, the rest tending to be about vanity or sex.*

Late summer is the hardest time for shearwater parents: they have a chick inside the burrow that is eating food at an almost insatiable rate in a race against a biological clock that insists the chick must be fully ready to fledge by the arrival of September. The rich diet of fish and cephalopods that gets regurgitated into its throat as the parents return from their foraging trips goes directly into growth, as its pre-digested form means that there is precious little waste. In the high summer, the chick will be gaining up to 15 grams of weight a day from the 50 grams that it eats and, to achieve this, the parents will need to deliver in excess of three kilos over the 70 days of its rearing.[3] That's not far short of four times their entire body weight, for each of them. And that's in addition to the amount they need to feed themselves. Towards the end of summer, the attentive parents have lost much of their own conditioning, which may be one of the stimuli that draws them southwards to a calmer, less crowded life.

....

* An assumption that has no basis in science or anything else, and which I offer to future students for free.

Happily, Manx shearwaters are not conscious of the various research papers written on their behalf, or else they would be dimly aware from the widely accepted theory of 'Ashmole's Halo' that the more successfully they feed in – and deplete – the seas around their islands, the more they are creating an artificial regulator for their own future population.[4] A gap slowly appears in the food supplies around the island, as the sources under the water are assaulted hour after hour by a million hungry birds. With seabirds tending to breed in enormous concentrations, a great example of the 'selfish herd' theory[5] whereby individual animals can consciously reduce their own personal risk by being part of a big group, it may also act as a self-imposed restriction on their ability to quickly breed themselves out of a decline. And it is the lack of available feeding at the end of the breeding season that ends up being the biggest incentive for the fledged chick to head southwards as soon as possible, rather than hanging around in the area perfecting its own fishing techniques. It is interesting to speculate exactly what is going on under the water in terms of fish stocks once the sky-full of birds leaves the island shores in late summer. I asked this question of one of the PhD students on Skomer the following month, and was impressed with the honesty and practicality of his answer.

'Dunno. Presumably more fish just turn up. You know, in the space left by the last lot.'

In a world of research papers it was somehow comforting to have such a spontaneous, un-peer-reviewed answer.

But right now, in this waning of the high northern summer, everything is about the building up of the strength to travel, and to travel far. Pelagic seabirds see the world map in the inverse way to us: where we see the comfort of our green land spaces edged by the blue of a hostile sea, they see vast oceans of relative security bordered by the hard and dangerous coast that they only need to brave so as to procreate. They are here in Britain partly because, at 12,429 km, we have one of the longest coastlines of any country in Europe, nearly twice that of Italy and three times that of France and Spain; and partly because it is just off the western coastline of the British Isles that the Atlantic conveyor belt system churns and recycles vast quantities of water from the depths up to the surface in a thousand-year process that hugely enriches the supply of seafood we share with the birds.

Ironically, the flickering lights of Mallaig twenty miles to the east, whose fishing community is facing a different battle for survival all of its own, will be the last land-based threat that a fledged shearwater will face as it wheels off the escarpment of Hallival for the very first time some rainy night in the next few weeks.

To an extent, the future success of the species depends on what happens next.

On an average early autumn day, you may be sharing the United Kingdom with around 400 million individual birds, of which a small fraction, possibly a million, may be shearwaters.[6] Be grateful for the deceptive simplicity of that figure: it took tens of thousands of hours of mainly voluntary work from the country's ornithologists to bring it to you.

Of the overall bird population, around a quarter will be made up of pheasants, wrens, blackbirds and robins, and the top ten species account for well over half of all birds. Counting bird populations accurately is by definition an inexact science, relying on estimates from sample counts, approved statistical techniques and assumptions about behaviour, and a whole range of other things. Generally, male birds are easier to count, as they tend to have brighter plumage and make more noise. Censuses normally only interest themselves in breeding pairs and, when it comes to Manx shearwaters, it involves playing taped calls down a sample of burrows and, quite literally, seeing who or what answers back.

The essence of counting bird numbers is to find out exactly what you *do* know, and then, rather like Donald Rumsfeld's 'known unknowns', extrapolate it across the half-known bits that you don't. And, when you do that, you eventually arrive at the conclusion that there are around 390,000 breeding pairs of Manx shearwaters (similar numbers to the moorhen, the oystercatcher and the linnet), and that they are in the 'common' category, the second of seven which starts at 'abundant' and finishes in 'extremely rare'. At the end of a good breeding season, there may be rather more than a million individuals in British airspace and down its earthy burrows, and it is fair to say that recent years have been quite kind to them. Kinder, at least, than they have been to many other seabirds.

Four hundred miles south of Rum, a far bigger concentration of shearwaters than I had ever seen were getting ready for their travels.

What was needed now, before the breeding season finally came to an end, was a visit to a tiny patch of sea off the south-west coast of Wales, and two little islands which, between them, are home to over half the world's Manx shearwaters. In a sense, that was where it had all started.

Small islands work well for breeding seabirds. Not only do the birds benefit individually from the 'safety in numbers' strategy in their huge colonies, but island populations tend to operate in a state of equilibrium[7] which allows researchers to understand much quicker than they otherwise might what is behind the rises and falls in populations. In order to attain a measure of biosecurity, and avoid the accidental introduction of that super-predator of seabirds, the rat, access to both Skomer and Skokholm is heavily restricted, especially for overnight stays. Which meant that Tim's invitation, given high up in the dark on Hallival, for me to spend time there with the researchers from the Oxnav group was a very useful one.

It also meant that I had about fourteen hours to drive through the night to get the tiny ferry over from Martin's Haven in Pembrokeshire.

For night was becoming my friend.

6. THE NIGHT VISITOR

September, Skomer Island

....

*The real voyage of discovery consists not in
seeking new landscapes, but in having new eyes.*
MARCEL PROUST

....

It was a fine life if you liked solitude, and eating rabbits.

And it was entirely in character for Ronald Lockley, tenant of a tiny and desolate island off the Welsh coast, to spend his honeymoon on Grassholm, an even tinier and more desolate one, eight miles further out into the Irish Sea. As it was the wilderness life that had attracted Doris to him in the first place, it was fine for his wife, too.

In 1927, and only a few years out of school, the young farmer who went on to become one of the fathers of modern British bird science took a 21-year lease on the island of Skokholm off the Pembrokeshire coast to see what he would

83

make of a life there. After a false start farming rabbits,* and after stripping a fortuitously arrived wreck, the *Alice Williams*, of wooden planks and beams for building materials, he made a home and set about his life's work of studying the wild-life around him, and particularly the seabirds. Frequently marooned for days on end by high winds, he and Doris grew, raised or made most of what they needed to subsist there, delighting in the privacy that it afforded their observations and lives. Lockley wrote more than 50 books and spent half a lifetime trying – and failing – to persuade the British govern-ment of the true environmental cost of a century of industrial development. But his towering achievement, the one left behind when all the others are riddled and sifted away by the passing years and the inexorable progress of science, is his twelve-year study of the Manx shearwater.

It was no accident that he became forever associated with the shearwater, as the island that he had chosen as his home, together with Skomer Island a couple of miles to its north, plays host to over 50% of their world population at any one time. Wherever he set his feet he would potentially be tripping over them and falling through into their burrows; Adam and Ada, his first study birds, had their burrow just a few feet from his back door. On occasion, when birds would crawl into the darkness under the floorboards or into the back of cupboards,

....

* He and his 1964 book *The Private Life of the Rabbit* became respectively the friendship and the inspiration behind Richard Adams' bestselling *Watership Down*, published in 1972, a book that, in turn, I read four times consecutively in 1973, and which inspired my first, last, and terrible attempt at a novel.

he didn't even have to leave the comfort of his own home to do the work. Through twelve long years of meticulous obser-vation and migrational experiments, on the ground, in their burrows, on the wing and far out at sea, he built up a picture that, 50 years before the first geolocator saw the light of day, still stands up pretty well to scientific scrutiny. With the help of men like David Lack and Geoffrey Matthews who still shine bright in the history of bird navigation science, his shearwaters were released all over the place like homing pigeons to estab-lish if, when and how quickly they would make it back to their burrows. Bit by bit, bird by bird, he put it all into a book that he published in 1942, and which still resonates across the decades today.

And it was a yellowing copy of this book that I was quietly reading in the small queue for the Skomer ferry on an early September morning. I half-remembered when I had been given it, aware that my grandmother had scoured the second-hand bookshops of Glasgow and Edinburgh for months to find it for me, but that my seventeenth birthday was probably not the right time for it. It had gone unceremoniously into my parents' bookshelves, and I hadn't clapped eyes on it for half a lifetime, up until the point where my sister and I were clearing out their house after they had both died.

She got the art books, I got history; she got gardening, I got politics; she got butterflies, I got birds, and that was why it had ended up with me. In our family, it was Roger who did birds, even when he didn't.

'That looks well loved,' said the man from the Valleys in the ferry queue behind me who had no right to be that cheerful so early in the morning. 'I was raised on that book back in the day. I come over here once a year, every year. For *him*, as much as for me.' He said the word 'him' as if referring to a minor deity, which, in a way, he was.

〜⁀〜

There is always something transformational about an island.

Islands are what you want them to be, even *who* you want them to be. They are 'where the imagination goes on holiday, ideals in physical form',* protected from ordinariness by the sea around them, and encouraging of dreams and fantasies from afar. For about ten years of my youth, just about every holiday we did was on an island – Wight in the early summer, Mull later, Mallorca occasionally – and the idea of them has never left me. It is not for nothing that so much of our lasting childhood literature involves them – *Treasure Island*, *Robinson Crusoe*, *Five On Kirrin Island Again*, *The Odyssey* – and as far as I was concerned, there would always be a potential cornucopia of parrots, pirates and buried treasure chests, even if they were only a couple of miles across the glittering Solent. To be surrounded by sea is to be just around the corner from an adventure.

Their defining isolation defies technology and still makes even the narrowest sea passage and the shortest stay equate to a little, discrete epic of travel. On the mainland, each mile that we journey might present a tiny evolution in the surroundings

....

* *The Summer Isles*, Philip Marsden (Granta, 2019).

and the people; the change provided by an island is stark and immediate, as if to cross that band of water is to move to another country and experience a different momentum. Islands, even ones like Skomer that are only a mile off the mainland, are, effectively, abroad. For me, they have always represented a 'beyondness' that instils a sense of adventure that I just don't have on the mainland. The effect is to make me feel that I have been away from home much longer than I actually have. Consequently, every other form of public transport becomes an opportunity to be silent and to read, whereas a boat trip tends to fill me with enthusiasm for the view, the seabirds and even my fellow travellers.

Islands are also what define the Manx shearwater's northern ranges and its summers. There are around 5,000 islands in the British archipelago, of which just 130 are permanently populated; just one of the populated ones, Rum, has breeding shearwaters on it in any numbers, and they are only there because they have stumbled on a high-altitude solution to foiling their predators, as we have seen. The shearwater has learned from experience that in parental life it is safer to be surrounded by sea, even if it is only a couple of miles away from a vast oil refinery, than it is on a mainland coast twenty miles from the nearest dwelling. In consequence of all this, the shearwater is restricted to around 45 islands off the west coast.

Compared to the crowds on Skomer at puffin time, we were a select gathering, and there turned out to have been no reason, other than the simple delight of hanging around in a fine place, for getting there early to queue. A small group from a Welsh university biology department were going to spend a day investigating the Skomer vole,* a BBC film cameraman was trying to get footage of seals, and my friend from the Valleys was on the first of his two island pilgrimages.

If you happen to choose a career studying – or writing about, for that matter – Manx shearwaters, one thing becomes abundantly clear very early on: you will be adding yourself to Britain's 3.2 million night-shift workers.[1] Other than the very stupid or very sick ones, the birds restrict their ground-based activities to a four- or five-hour period around midnight, and if you want to observe them closely, then those are the hours that you too must keep, as I had discovered on Rum. With black-backed gulls, ravens, and buzzards around every island colony that they inhabit, it is just too risky for them to be out and about when predators are still in the air. To make things just that little bit more challenging, the conditions they prefer during those dark hours are moonless, windy ones that are just a little bit wet – everything, in fact, that an average adult human has spent years trying to avoid. Before and after those times, all is quiet and, to the uninitiated, you may well believe yourself to be in the centre of the world's largest rabbit warren, rather than a vast seabird colony. This also explains why the only sound I could hear from the Oxnav team when I jumped enthusiastically off the morning boat and presented myself at their hut were deep snores, which

....

* The Skomer vole (*Myodes glareolus skomerensis*) appears to have been introduced accidentally to the island by boat, and has thrived ever since, to the point that there are now around 20,000 of them. Having spent a millennium or more with no mammal predators to worry about, they have a completely different fright reflex (staying very still) than the mainland ones (run like hell). I love that.

gave me an excuse to spend an hour watching biology students giving frights to voles at the other side of the island.

The Oxnav team, approaching season's end, were manically busy trying to bring to a meaningful conclusion the eight or nine research experiments that they had been running over the course of the summer. Gradually, they woke up, ingested unfeasible amounts of coffee, and then explained what they were up to and what I could expect to find.

'Most of them have fledged* by now,' said Joe, one of the two PhD students, 'so we are just dealing with the last of our study birds.' Then he saw the alarm in my face at the thought that I might have missed the proverbial boat, and added: 'There were probably 200,000 chicks in the colony, so there's still 50,000 or so left. But from the point of view of our research, it's really just the phase for tidying it all up before we go back to Oxford and spend the winter doing the quantitative stuff, and getting it all down on paper.'

From a high point in late June, the general seabird busyness of an island like Skomer dies down gradually to a point in mid-September when the sky around the island seems to be just for the gannets, gulls and shags. Gone are the puffins out into the Atlantic and the guillemots and razorbills out to the open seas further north. Stretches of water that would have contained a dense carpet of birds flying above or swimming on them two months ago are eerily empty, almost as if something

---

* Fledging is the point at which the soft down that the chick is born with has been replaced by a full set of flight feathers, and the youngster flies from its birthplace.

has gone wrong and there has been some unreported disaster. There hasn't. All that has happened is that the pelagic seabirds have once again asserted the annual truth that they are birds of the oceans, not the rocks, and that their natural element is out among the waves. And, if the sky belongs to the gannets, the seashores are the fiefdom of the grey seal, and the quiet is punctuated by the haunting whines and howls of the hungry pups.

I quickly grew into the island routine on my short stay, just happy to be in my new upside-down world where a man on the brink of his 60th birthday was the office junior for five graduates and undergraduates, none of whom was older than 26. After a few housework jobs to prove that I at least wanted to be useful, I participated in the concluding part of a small experiment to weigh the last five remaining study birds, all of whom were due to fledge in the next day or two. Because shearwaters tend to nest in burrows that are often longer than the human arm, most of the burrows in the study area had a shorter, man-made entrance immediately above the resident chick, which meant that the bird could be removed with minimal disturbance. I watched the process for the first two chicks, and was then allowed to do the third myself.

I lay tight on the grassy hillside in the late summer sunshine and pushed my right arm down into the hole until I was touching the back of the chick, a female. Terrified that I would somehow injure her through my innate clumsiness, I clasped her around the chest and gradually worked her uphill, backwards, into the daylight, trying to make sure that neither wing nor leg caught on the side of the burrow. There, off the Pembrokeshire coast, a mere 31 days since that other bird had flown back into my life off the Isle of Rum, I found myself holding a shearwater, scarcely able to believe that something so small, so light and so seemingly fragile was itself on the brink of a trans-oceanic flight of 8,000 miles. No parents, no guidance, no second chance if it all went wrong. The only other things that fly 8,000 miles between continents tend to weigh 400 tons and be powered by 1,800 brake horsepower engines. The thought of a creature no bigger than the collared dove that regularly visited the bird table outside my kitchen window doing a journey of this scale was astonishing. I thought back to the night that I had wandered around my house trying to find something that weighed around 400 grams, and remembered the Evelyn Waugh novel. On balance, the *Sword of Honour* trilogy looked decidedly robust compared to what I was holding.

Once out, I put the bird into a black felt bag, weighed her at 440 grams and slipped her back into the burrow. The weight, high enough to be healthy, but low enough to show that she hadn't been fed recently, together with the general air of well-being and the lack of any infant down, suggested that she was in her last couple of days on the island. On her right leg was a geolocator that, some time far into the future, would tell the next generation of Oxford biology students just what she had been up to in the intervening years. Between now and then, there would be only silence from Bird T72.* Lines of latitude and longitude would be crossed and recrossed, coastlines and

....

* The Oxnav study birds are identified by individual numbers stuck in the ground at the head of their burrows. T72 is one of them, a pseudonym, to protect her identity. She is the inheritor of a Lockley tradition that goes back to RS2246 and RS2256 (Ada and Adam) in 1929.

storms avoided, fishing grounds discovered, but it would be an anonymous life, and a largely solitary one.

Migration waits for no man, and Joe knew that he and the team had a maximum of another week before the opportunities to work with the birds dwindled away.

———⌒———

Lockley's work certainly started something.

Up until the latter half of the twentieth century, the vast majority of what we knew about pelagic seabirds came from mainly observational work done in and around their breeding grounds and seasons, with the other seven or eight months a mystery. Out at sea, they might be spotted from lighthouses or ships – whose presence they have always regarded as a good source of a meal – or their ringed corpses collected from some distant beach, but fundamentally their ocean lives were their own. Ringing projects, which had been carried out for scientific purposes only since the beginning of the twentieth century in an attempt to find out about bird populations and breeding success, became formalised with the founding of the British Trust for Ornithology (BTO) around the time that Lockley took on the lease of Skokholm Island. The reason that Callum had known roughly where the Manx shearwater went in the northern winter all those years ago was probably no more than the aggregated result of a very large amount of observation by a very large number of sailors.

From the 1950s onwards, scientists toyed with VHF transmitters which, while good with large and localised animals, were rendered next to useless on seabirds by the distances involved and the fact that they needed line of sight to work, an option denied by birds spending a good deal of their time behind waves. By the early 1990s, technology had enabled platform terminal transmitters (PTTs) to be attached to albatrosses and, while far from perfect, the messages coming in via the Argos fast satellite tracking system* helped to produce rough migratory maps over a one- or two-year period. Suddenly, we found out, for example, that the wandering albatross would make standard feeding trips of up to 15,000 km (not far off the distance the average car driver travels in a year), circulating the globe for a meal or two – and that was just the start of it. The pace has quickened in the last twenty years or so, particularly in respect of GPS,† which can feed back real-time information on, say, a bird in the South Atlantic to a scientist in Edinburgh or Fremantle. The future of bird tracking seems to be partly in outer space, where the Icarus‡ project uses the International Space Station to re-broadcast signals from the tags of earthbound animals and birds, and partly using the 5G (and subsequent) elements of the mobile phone system.

Where the bird goes is one thing, but what it does on its way and when it gets there is quite another. Electronic salt

....

* Argos is a network of satellites supporting environmental studies, which use the angle and pitch of the signals received to determine positions with a fair degree of accuracy (BTO).

† Global Positioning System. This technology gives high-precision fixes on a real-time basis. Its disadvantage has been, until recently, its cost and its appetite for battery life.

‡ International Cooperation for Animal Research Using Space.

water immersion loggers, for example, which can now be built into the 2-gram geolocator ring on the bird's leg,* can tell us how long the bird is spending on the water, and give details of each and every dive; and wet-dry sensors can start to feed back information on how long they have spent submerged (i.e. fishing), and at what depth. Temperature sensors can be deployed into a bird's stomach which, by detecting the changes in stomach temperature, can tell us exactly when it has eaten and, in combination with the depth gauges, how deep down it went to get the meal in the first place. We now know, for example, that an emperor penguin regularly fishes 100 metres down, and has even been recorded five times deeper than that. And by knowing how deep they go, we begin to understand what they will be feeding on and therefore under what degree of threat they are living their lives. Down below, as up above, there is a highly sensitive food chain; so when the sea around Scotland warms half a degree, for example, the weight of available plankton for the sand eels reduces and moves away, and, in indirect consequence, the puffin population crashes by 40%.

Nowadays, scientists can even attach tiny GoPro cameras to the back of birds' heads, which can produce extraordinary images of how they swim – or fly – underwater, how they interact with other 'anglers' down there, and the kinds of events that send them deep down in the first place. Revelation by revelation, by knowing what they are doing and how, we have slowly but

....

* Accepted industry practice says that the total weight of any single or combined device being carried by a bird should not exceed 3% of its normal body weight, not an ideal that I remember the army putting into effect on behalf of infantrymen like me.

surely come to understand the threats they face, and how we can best persuade our restless world to look after them. Added to which, our observation and knowledge drives our understanding in other areas; the shearing flights of albatrosses and shearwaters, for example, are already informing and influencing the design of drones and unmanned aircraft.[2] And long before they did that, the basic structure of a bird's wing (convex above, concave below, thick and strong at the forward edge, thin and flexible at the trailing edge) inspired the basic design of an aircraft wing, where the lift is provided by the air travelling further and faster over the upper surface of the wing than the lower, and where the leading edge is higher than the trailing edge.[3]

~~~

It is all a far cry from 1936, when Lockley persuaded a group of students and their teacher, who had been staying with him on Skokholm, to take three shearwaters, three storm petrels and six puffins back to Devon on the train to see if they happened to know how to come back. Unsurprisingly, most of them died in their hampers on the journey, but his favourite, the old and much-married Caroline, made it back to her burrow by midnight, having been released only ten hours earlier in Dartington. One storm petrel and one puffin also made it back. All the Devon party knew for certain was that Caroline had flown southwards (the wrong direction for Skokholm, but the right one for the nearest bit of sea) and out of their lives. This left tantalisingly open the matter of how she had made it back, by what route and with what resources.

Lockley's obsession with ringing and homing burgeoned from there. A few weeks later, he released two of his Skokholm birds from a ship near the Faroe Islands (600 miles north), and then took a Faroes bird away with him and released it from Edinburgh. All returned to their burrows successfully. Then he sent shearwater RW9915 to the Castle of Mey in northern Scotland (success) and a couple to Le Havre (ditto) before famously packing two off to Venice, one of which returned to the island fourteen days later 'fat and glossy'. Lockley's supposition was that the bird had overflown the narrowest parts of Italy and France, and that it had an instinctive understanding of what direction its home lay in.

In the cause of science, his shearwaters were also released from Frensham Ponds in Surrey, Limerick (where an obliging guard allowed his train to be stopped on the Shannon Bridge to perform the release) and even 5,300 feet up in the landlocked Alps. Each time, the bird made it home, but it is striking that Lockley really learned nothing more than that shearwaters could home. Even a dispassionate conservationist might raise an eyebrow at some of his later experiments: for example, all three birds died in the boat that was taking them to Cape Town before they even got to the equator, and three were unceremoniously lobbed out of a biplane 2,000 feet above Stratford-upon-Avon. In fact, being one of Lockley's favourites, the birds he always seemed to use for his experiments, would have been very much a mixed blessing, as they often spent as much time on public transport as they did down their burrows. Lockley finally wrote with some honesty that his 'experiments with shearwaters failed to explain the mechanisms of homing'.

And yet the science was assuredly on the move, both in its scope and its rigour, and it led inexorably to the library roof in Cambridge seventeen years later.

The Oxnav team I was being allowed to visit were Lockley's direct inheritors, and only a couple of miles from where he did most of his work. Importantly for me, the science I was starting to get involved with was as a world away from the sterile school laboratory experiments on locusts I was doing 50 years ago. Back at school, science had been defined by white coats, smoky test-tubes and exams I never passed; out in the wild, it was T-shirts, beards* and adventure. The field research they were doing out there in the pitch dark was building ever more on a knowledge base as divergent as wing muscle development, magnetic influences, orientation, threats from light pollution, and the hierarchy of inputs into their sense of navigation. On its own, each component of study seemed almost impossibly specialist, but aggregated with all the others, and then across all the other animal species that are being researched by other teams in other locations, it is a pyramid of knowledge that allows David Attenborough to deliver his grave one-liners to a mass audience with utter conviction, and year by year for the rest of us to understand our natural world ever better.

---

* Actually, most zoology undergraduates that I met working on seabirds were female, so the beard is becoming a rarity again.

All those years, and all that science, also enabled me to enter the life of a bird that has been researched and monitored so extensively that even a novice like me could know as much about an individual shearwater as I did about my son at university, and for a whole lot less outlay. Rather more, in fact, even if they both kept similar hours, as the latter made a better fist of the maintenance of his privacy.

Deep in her burrow just before midnight on Wednesday, Bird T72 is forcing herself with a paddle motion up to the entrance hole and out into the Pembrokeshire night.

Her parents, attentive feeders that they have been on her behalf up until a couple of weeks ago, have finally stopped visiting her, as a result of which she has gone from being half again as heavy as them in mid-August down to their own weight now, just over 400 grams, the point at which the biomechanics of flight will work for her.* During this time, and with a great deal of help from her own preening, her down has been replaced by her flight feathers, and she has developed from a comically circular fluffy chick into the sleek black and white adult bird. She is very hungry, but she knows there is nothing for her here.

Her senses are fully developed by now. Like all seabirds, her eyesight is a compromise between seeing ahead and laterally

....

* Much work has been done on the trigger for migration, starting with Victorian caged birds being observed to be extra restless, and to be gaining weight, at a particular time of year.

only as well as she has to, and chasing prey under water; for a bird that operates extensively at night, her eyes are not particularly well adapted for darkness, but she can get by. She hears well enough to recognise her parents' calls as they fly in towards the burrow to feed her, as one day her own chicks will recognise hers. The olfactory bulb within her brain is bigger, relatively, than almost any other bird, which gives some indication how important the sense of smell will be to her, both in locating food and in finding her way back to Skomer when the time comes. Although birds have only about a hundredth of the taste buds that humans do, she can distinguish between different food types, even if we don't yet know if she can discriminate between ones she prefers and ones she tolerates. It is far too crude to call it an inbuilt compass, but, finally, she has a strong magnetic awareness, familiar to all birds, that will make a telling contribution to her coming travels.

Is she intelligent? Certainly not in the sense of cunning like the raven, or in terms of memory, like the jay, or mimicry, like the mynah bird; but, as we will see, she can adapt, plan and negotiate, and she can use her hooked bill as a useful enough tool. Lockley once watched great shearwaters in Portugal preventing their eggs from rolling away from their cave nests by importing hundreds of tiny round pebbles with which to create the effect of a bowl.

For the past four or five evenings, T72 has made this journey, drawn out of her safe burrow by the twin imperatives, beyond that of hunger, of gathering sensory information from the world around her, and flapping the wings that she knows will be the key to her travels, an exercise she can't do underground. She may stop for a while at the entrance to the burrow and just look up and out, as if getting her bearings. Each night, she has gone a little further than the night before, propelling herself along and upwards by a mixture of wings, feet and beak, always looking to be as high as she can climb without going further than she is comfortable with. In the moonlight, her struggling form might seem to be some cruel evolutionary prank, and even a predator as inept as man can intercept and pick her up by simply stooping down. Yet she is not one of Britain's more successful seabirds for nothing.

If her burrow is in tall vegetation such as bracken, she will head for open ground, almost as if the paths are runways for her. When she gets there, she will not be alone. On a busy night, there may be another bird every two or three yards.

She will do anything for those extra inches of height – a boulder, a fallen gate-post, a dry-stone wall, a fellow shearwater, even a loose clump of undergrowth – for it is height, as well as breeze, that instinct tells her is what she needs for the start of the next part of her life.

When she meets an obstacle that she finds she can't climb, a small rucksack for example, her personal safety often plays little or no part in how she reacts. Sure, she might crash off into the undergrowth with a noisy whirring of those yet-to-be-elegant wings, but she is more likely to sit there until the danger is past, before continuing on her way. The sea is calling out to her, sending her signals that she cannot much longer ignore.

On Skomer she is lucky. There are no rats, foxes, stoats or other mammalian predators on the island, and the birds that would make short work of her in daylight don't usually fly at night. This is just as well, as not only is her progress rather tortuous, but it is far from silent, punctuated, as it is, by a mixture of childish 'cheeps' and haunting adult calls. Meanwhile, her only weapon is her beak; evolved as an efficient tool for fishing, it would be no match for any determined aggressor. It all comprises a strange set of circumstances that has still somehow allowed her species' population on both Skomer and Skokholm to multiply considerably since Lockley's days while most other seabirds have suffered long-term declines. The biggest influence on seabird populations is the ready availability of food, and she just happens to feed on a mixture that does not yet seem to have been overly affected by the warming oceans.

After about 70 or 80 yards, she stops, appears to think for a moment, and then turns around to make her noisy, ungainly way back to her burrow. Instinctively, she knows she needs a good breeze so she can take off, but not so much that it will be difficult for her to land on the sea. Maybe it is the stillness of the night, maybe the bright moonlight, but something tells her that it is not tonight. Tonight, she will be back where she has been for the previous 70 nights, even though there is movement and departure all around her.

A quarter of an hour later, she is deep in her burrow preening the final tiny pieces of down from the bottom of her breast. After a while, she sleeps, the last static sleep she will know for the next thousand days.

From tomorrow, she will be a bird in almost constant motion.

The ethical guidelines in bird science have moved on quite a bit since Lockley's day. He had already been, after all, an unwitting assassin of a number of the birds he adored by shipping them around the world in friends' suitcases, not to mention accidentally char-grilling a couple when he experimented with burning an area of grass.

But by sustained observation over many nights, in early September of his first full year on Skokholm, he was beginning to close in on the mystery surrounding fledging. He knew, but didn't know why, the parents abandoned the chick in the weeks before; he knew that they needed a handful of nights' practice to orientate themselves outside the burrow and exercise their wings; he knew that they used all five 'limbs' (feet, wings and hooked beak) to scramble up on high points; and he knew that most of the early flights ended in the dull thud of earthbound failure. But when he tired of the things he didn't know, he would take matters into his own hands in a way that would fail the first ethical hurdle these days: 'I tried encouraging them by throwing some as forcibly and as high as I could into the eye of the wind.' Then he is collecting up a basket full of them and taking them down to the sea to short-circuit the first flight altogether. Ignoring his wife's maternal cries of 'They're too young, Ronald!', he floats, drops and throws them out into the water to see if they can swim straight away, which they can, dive straight away, ditto, and fish straight away, probably. But he is still miles away from comprehending the full significance of that first flight. 'If we could have followed Hoofti* and his

....

* Offspring of Adam and Ada, Lockley's earliest shearwater couple.

fellow fledglings out to sea that autumn, we should have been glad,' he wrote. 'We were very curious to see how they behaved at sea, and where they migrated to.'[4]

After nightfall, I went to the other side of Skomer with three of the research team to participate in the conclusion of different experiments designed to establish the degree to which shearwaters might be deceived into flying towards artificial light, such as the tankers out in the bay, and the influences on their sense of orientation, and hence direction, if you were to put them in an artificially strange place and leave them to it. Each experiment, in order to be valid for research purposes and be eventually peer-reviewed, needed to be done multiple times in a series of different locations, so there was an added note of urgency about this particular night's work.

It was a world utterly changed from the daylight one we had been working in earlier. Even at this late stage of the season, there were birds on the ground everywhere, shuffling their awkward way down the paths, butting into passing boots and searching for that little bit of extra height that would bring welcome breeze to the underside of their wings. In 50 years of watching birds I had seen nothing remotely like this night-time mass exodus. It seemed to have more in common with turtle hatchlings propelling themselves down some moonlit tropical beach towards the gleam of the sea below than it did with familiar bird behaviour. The red head torches we carried, so as not to dazzle the birds we were working with, lent an other-worldly tone to our very limited view of the distance, where the red eyes of Skomer's many rabbits indicated in just what close proximity these two species operated.

Catching the birds was really quite simple, although the feistier they were (these tended to be the really healthy ones we wanted to use in the tests) the more they would hurtle back into the cover of the bracken, only to be followed seconds later by 75 kilos of research student diving horizontally in after them. Or 87 kilos of me. For statistical relevance many birds were needed for each site, so it wasn't long before I too was plunging blind over dry-stone walls and crashing around in the undergrowth, before delicately collecting the chick and getting it into the safety of a felt bag.

'Am I really doing this?' I asked myself silently as I took a breather on a little boulder, clutching my three full bags. The night was moving on, and my colleagues were running their tests, all the while making observations in their well-thumbed notebooks by the gentle light of a head torch. A life that had relatively recently consisted of sitting in a well-lit office, visiting customers and walking around trade shows; that had included endless travel, half-decent meals and the creation of international trading relationships; that involved looking as smart as I needed to, to do what I did as well as I could – had I traded it all for diving around the undergrowth at one o'clock in the morning in an island full of strange noises, covered in bracken dust and, not to put too fine a point on it, seabird shit?

I had, and like a rediscovery of childhood, I had never been professionally happier in my life. A layer of seabird shit was a small price to pay.

As I stood stiffly up in the night to make my way back to the other end of the island and my sleeping bag, approximately 440 grams of fast-moving bones, flesh and feathers struck me sharply on the left side of the head, an outcome that I had been warned was odds-on, and which in some respects I suppose I was secretly looking forward to. In the event, I'm not sure who was more surprised, the bird or me, but we both picked ourselves up and continued to do what we had been doing before we met.

As I made my lone way back down the bird-strewn pathways, the lights of Milford Haven oil refinery over in the east, I reflected a bit more on the significance of this sharp turn in the direction of my life. Approaching the age of 60 was generally a time for settling down, for doing what you did as well as you possibly could in preparation for the still-disguised benefits of retirement out there on the near horizon. Words like 'pension', 'cruise' and 'winding down' were supposed to be the currency of conversation, not 'uncertainty', 'learning' and 'night-work', let alone being thumped into by half-kilo birds. My family and friends were thankfully supportive of this new round-peg-in-round-hole aura; they could spot someone working with the grain of his character just as easily as I could. Sometimes, I could just about feel my grandmother's hands in the small of my back, pushing me gently towards the lonely acres of empty ocean that my shearwaters were headed for. 'You're damn lucky to have the chance,' she would say, cutting through any hesitation I might have about joining the adventure. 'So just get on and do it while you still can.'

Impostor syndrome it may well have been, but it all gave me quiet confidence that I was a lot closer to earning the right to grow that beard than when I had arrived.

On the Thursday, Bird T72 paddles her way once again up to the entrance of her burrow, only a little earlier than the previous evening. Long before she emerges, she can sense the changes in the world above, the slight damp in the air and the increased breeze. This is her sixth night of movement and of exploration. Whatever else she knows, and it is little, she knows that her time as an underground creature is coming to an end.

Propelling herself along the same path in the same direction, she flaps her wings and pushes with her webbed feet with more commitment than before, and finally manages to force her way up onto the broken-down wall that had defeated her on the two previous nights.

Right alongside her is another shearwater, its black and white head staring out at the nothingness at the other side of the wall, the side where the breeze is coming from. Along the wall are other birds, but they are not what she is thinking about, other than the possibility of gaining an inch or two by climbing on top of them.

The lights of the Pembrokeshire coastline in front of her, and of the empty oil tankers riding out against the flood tide in St Brides Bay are well defined on this moonless night, but she is not confused by them. She already knows which way she will turn when she rises up in the air.

Finally, she stands up slightly on her set-back feet, facing the wind, and flaps her wings as hard as she can. Instinct, the only commodity she can call upon in the absence of her parents, urges her to greater and greater efforts until she suddenly rises up into the night sky, catches the breeze and leaves the wall, up into the darkness.

Everything she has ever known has left her life the instant she commits herself to the darkness, wind and air above her, and for now she is guided only by the instructions within the genetic coding that she was born with. Her parents communicated none of this to her in those dark and watchful July and August days at the base of the burrow; they merely kept her safe and fed until some inner signal told them to leave her to fend for herself.* Over the coming days, she may mingle with other Skomer shearwaters and they will perhaps all learn from observation, but right now, somewhere in the night sky above the sea, she is utterly committed to a future about whose promises she has not the faintest clue.

Behind her is the burrow, and the tidy life she has known until now. In three or four years, she will probably come back to that very spot as the starting point for her own breeding life,[5] but with the wind under her wings, that is the last thing on her mind. She may tarry for a day or two, especially if she is confused by, say, a lighthouse,[6] but with the fish stocks around her island now depleted – which is probably why her parents headed south when they did – a dynamic urgency exists.

She is hungry, and she has far to travel.

~⁊~

....

* Shearwaters are dependent on their parents for around 0.5% of their natural lives, in sharp contrast to humans, where the figure is around 20%, 40 times longer.

A few hours later, everything had changed for me too.

The overnight weather forecast had revealed an intensified northerly wind for the next four days, which would make landing in the exposed harbour impossible for the ferry, meaning that anyone who needed to be off the island in the next week, needed to do so this morning. That meant three of the five researchers, and most of the heavy equipment, had to leave three days early, and in a hurry. If one of the features of following shearwaters was the night-shift, another was the permanent uncertainty of island weather and available boats. Man may well have put people on the moon, but back on earth he is still grappling with four-foot swells and windward landing sites.

While we were packing up, we took a moment to watch the sun rise over Milford Haven, just as people had been doing on Skomer for millennia. It was an emotional time. Even though the cast list of students had changed over the summer, my new friends had spent the last hectic weeks living their night-time shifts cheek by jowl with each other, sharing confidences and building deep relationships. Their commitment to accurate research, and above all to that bird, was extraordinary, and no one could blame them for a moment or two of reflection as it all drew to its premature close.

For five minutes or so, no one really said anything, but then nothing needed saying. For my own part, I had only been there for a few days but it felt like more. Whatever the private thoughts that the others were lost in, mine were simple.

Somewhere out there, beyond the lightening southern horizon, I thought, Bird T72 is starting her long journey across the sea, first stop who knows where.

And somewhere high up in my pre-frontal cortex, a complex justification was being created for a rather expensive air ticket in the same direction.

7. TOWARDS A
SOUTHERN OCEAN

Autumn, Mid–Atlantic

....

*The idea of wilderness needs no
defense, it only needs defenders.*
EDWARD ABBEY

....

My grandmother's cottage was the central point of an intricate web of sometimes surprising relationships.

She had at least six locals who came round on a regular basis: Monday was for Morag, who cleaned; Tuesday was for Ian the Park, who largely drank whisky behind the shed; Wednesday for Rosie, Thursday for John and Friday back to Morag again. Down the way were the 'boys' in the Ardfenaig Hotel, a couple whom she adored, protected and tutted at in equal measure, and dotted around the place were people like Joan (with whom she polished and sold Iona stones) and

Margaret (who was a bit racy, and gave her highly unsuitable novels to read). Further afield was her bookmaker in London, to whom, wreathed in a cloud of Turkish tobacco smoke, she would make long post-breakfast calls so as to attend to the important business of laying the daily bets. It is astounding that she managed to do this effectively. Newspapers were always a day old when they arrived at the Bayview Stores, and the internet was no more than a faint concept in the mind of a young physics undergraduate at Queen's College, Oxford, so she had to rely on the weekly racing digest *Timeform*.

She wasn't rich, by any means, but she was comfortable. And what she lacked in pension, she made up by being an inveterate speculator in gold which was, to her way of thinking, a robust certainty in an otherwise dishonest world. For a reason no one could quite work out, she seemed to know instinctively when to buy, to hold and to sell, and she ended up with a stack of Krugerrands and sovereigns under her mattress for when 'the balloon went up'. And when it never did, she started passing these down the family to people who largely thought that she had been out of her mind investing in them in the first place.

Then there were those letters, endlessly banged out on that faithful typewriter. There were letters of news to her southern friends, letters of 'salutary correction' to her grandchildren, letters of encouragement to a legion of people she supported, and – above all – letters to politicians and churchmen of a left-leaning persuasion with whom she profoundly disagreed. Mind you, you didn't need to be particularly left-wing for her to regard you as such: anywhere beyond the middle part of the

Tory party would do. For a while, she had a rather character-less Alsatian called 'Mr Smith' after the beleaguered leader of a country that she could never bring herself to call Zimbabwe. All those letters were in her trademark font, and all were borne away on her behalf by ex-England goalkeeper turned Bunessan postman, Peter 'The Cat' Bonetti, with whom she shared a deep mutual affection and an occasional card school. I suspect that my grandmother had never heard of him or his sporting achievements before he arrived on her doorstep in a Royal Mail uniform; and I suspect, too, that it was this honest ignorance that he most cherished in her.

If there was an antonym to the concept of virtue signalling, it would have belonged to my grandmother. Her stated views on many things would rightly have her banned from public platforms these days, but in practice, she was driven by a quiet Christianity that made her support the vulnerable as much as she promoted the underdog. It was the privileged and powerful who were mostly lined up in her sights – wreckers, as she saw it, who had spoiled an imperial heritage that many of her friends had died for. 'She said her prayers,' said the minister, years later at her funeral, 'and she meant them.' Only after she had died, and when her papers were being cleared up, did we fully understand how many standing orders she had for charities and her 'lame ducks'. In her will she bequeathed to me, in addition to some sentimental bits and pieces from her mantle-piece, an annoying moral obligation to go on looking after two abused donkeys at a sanctuary in Somerset. I did so for years, until Caroline proved conclusively to me that the original 'Barney' and 'Clover', on whose behalf my grandmother had signed up in the first place, had died years ago and were simply being recycled in photographic form whenever renewal time was up. It turned out that she could live with people taking her for a ride much more than she could live without campaigning, which was what got her out of bed in the morning and had the rest of us occasionally ducking for cover.

The obvious effect of a childhood's exposure to all this was to make me question just about everything, all the time, and to ensure that at no time did I lack a campaign of my own in which to pitch my energies. The less obvious one was to push me out into the wide world as soon as I could get there, in order to see things for myself. If, as Nietzsche was fond of asserting, 'there are no facts, only interpretations', she had taught me always to use personal experience as the acid test.

But the one bequest that couldn't come off that mantlepiece was her restless fascination with the world around her. That, I absorbed over two and a half decades along with the Turkish tobacco smoke. And it was that restlessness which was now calling me thousands of miles to the south-south-west.

—⁊—

Normally, when we sate our fascination by travel, we journey to fixed points. The destinations are known.

I already clearly understood that shearwaters don't work like that outside the breeding season. They are creatures of freedom who acknowledge no postcodes or conveniently fixed destinations. They fly between 50 and 200 miles a day in search of food, even when they are not on their migration.

Argentina has a coastline of 3,118 miles, and a distance out to the continental shelf (beyond which my birds would tend not to go during the southern summer) that averages out at around 225 miles.

The easy bit was paying £396 plus assorted air miles for a return flight to Buenos Aires. Rather harder would be searching the resulting 750,000 square miles of ocean for a rapidly moving and well camouflaged target when I got there. Doing it in a language I could hardly speak, off a continent I had never set foot on, and with a constitution that only had to look at a boat to feel sick, just made the adventure more compelling.

'I cannot commit to anything,' emailed the first sea tour company when I contacted them to see if I could join one of their trips. 'The weather is normally too rough, our politics is horrible, and our economy is very, very bad.'

'This is not possible,' said the second. 'Maybe I will be sailing the weekend you are here. I hope it.'

'The boat is not so good,' replied the third, with uncompromising honesty. A subsequent look at what passed as his website was enough to foster the impression that both he and his boat had utterly lost interest in the future.

This was going to be more of a challenge than I had first anticipated.

When Bird T72 rose up from her dry-stone wall that September night, she oriented herself against the moonless gleam of the water and turned south-west towards the open sea. From now on, just as dry land would be her anathema, the wind would be her element.

Until October 19th, 1952, when a Skokholm-ringed bird was found freshly dead on a beach in southern Brazil, it was assumed that they wintered in the western Atlantic rather than the south. After that, a map based on other recovered birds slowly starting emerging, indicating that the vast majority of British birds were wintering off the Brazilian and Argentine coast, staying there till late January and then heading back by a very different route. And, however quickly they chose to make the outward journey, the route down to the west African coast was always pretty much the same: Scilly Isles, Bay of Biscay (where local fishermen routinely caught and ate them until the late 1970s*), and then off the coasts of Portugal, Morocco and Western Sahara. And they weren't just eaten on their travels: Basque fishermen would shoot and dissect them, and then set their nets according to what fish were in the birds' stomachs. Ronald Lockley once wrote of a shearwater's ringed leg and foot that had been discovered in the belly of a small fish that had in turn been eaten by a 40-pound anglerfish, caught off a pier in Brittany: when he read the number on the ring, RV7507, he was distressed to identify it as one of his favourites, a bird that had set distance records for him the previous year.

It was found that after passing the bulge of Africa the routes diverged, depending on the individual bird. Some would

....

* A recent professional seabird tasting trial awarded the shearwater 6.5 out of 10, in a league propped up by the oily shag at 4.0. All in all, though, human consumption remains one of its lesser problems.

fly on south down the African coast to Angola and then head due west with the trade winds while others, the majority perhaps, cut across just below the shortest 2,500-mile hop over the southern Atlantic from Senegal to Natal and Recife in Brazil. While 2,500 miles is a long way for a human, it is a mere five-day journey to a bird that flies at 30 miles per hour and doesn't stop much. Also, recent research has hinted at, but not proved, the idea that each chick tends to choose the route its parents chose, flying down at the general rate, and with the same foraging routine, that they did.

The unconscious genius behind this migration lies in the birds' instinctive understanding of the different trade winds and gyres of the two parts of the Atlantic. Overlay the map of a Manx shearwater's migratory route down to South America on a chart of the Portuguese mariners from 500 years ago, and you will likely get an eerie similarity. Both parties understood the effects of the South and North Atlantic gyres perfectly. Neither wanted to travel straight into the wind, so neither ever did. Down south, where the gyre goes anti-clockwise across the shortest passage and down the length of the South American coast, that's where T72 will make her crossing. Up north, where it circles clockwise past the Caribbean, the US east coast and Newfoundland, that is the way she will eventually make her way back when she is ready to head for her breeding grounds.

Most young shearwaters seem to take their time heading south, stopping occasionally in proven fishing grounds to raft up socially for up to two weeks at a time on the sea with other birds and re-provision. Others travel as fast as they reasonably can, pulled southwards by the lengthening days, the height of the sun, the position of the stars and the smells of the ocean.* One studied bird, for example, travelled 139 continuous hours at an average speed of 55 kph on his way south, effectively two thirds of his journey.[1] The bird found dead on a beach in Brazil in 1952 was discovered just sixteen days after it had been ringed in Skokholm. Given that the finder reckoned it had been dead for three days, it is likely that it had made the trip at the astonishing rate of 500 or 600 miles a day, every day, and had rarely if ever stopped.[2]

The question, of course, that has enthralled scientists and researchers for decades is just how the birds do it. And not just shearwaters, but the other oceanic wanderers. And not just the oceanic wanderers, but all the pigeons, storks, cranes, divers, geese, nightingales, swallows and songbirds that chase down those faraway seasons twice a year, every year. The answer, rather obviously, starts in understanding that bird navigation is very much not a one-size-fits-all science, and that each species, sometimes each sub-species, is bound by a different set of inputs.[†] For at least 60 years, and using a bewildering array of equipment and ingenuity, science has gradually built up a picture of how it is the Manx shearwater knows where to go; how it is, for example, that one of Lockley's birds was released on the eastern perimeter of Boston's Logan Airport in 1952

....

* Other birds have even more extreme journeys. The 250-gram bartailed godwit, for example, goes from Alaska to New Zealand and back (7,000 miles) in one go.

† An entire sub-section of animal science has specialised in this subject for decades, and the reading material is plentiful. A good, readable start is Michael Brooke's *Far From Land* (Princeton University Press, 2018).

and still made it back to its burrow on Skokholm before the letter notifying its safe release arrived. Even now, most of the scientists involved see the picture as only just beginning to be understood, and there are experiments going on all the time to further refine the knowledge.

The recipe card for navigation in a seabird is an extensive one, comprising a mix of sun, stars, magnetic pull, homing instinct, sight, sound, smell and memory. Each experiment, over those 60 years, has had to limit itself to assessing the relative importance of just one of those elements against just one of the others, or against a control. So back in 1953, when Geoffrey Matthews released those birds from the roof of the Cambridge library, it was basically an exercise in proving orientation ability. Fast forward 60 years, and Professor Anna Gagliardo's experiments of 2010 and 2011,[3] in which a third of the study birds (Cory's shearwaters) released 500 miles out into the Atlantic had their olfactory cells temporarily disabled by a zinc sulphate solution, a third had a tiny magnet glued to their head feathers to disable magnetic navigation, and a third were untouched control birds, showed that the control and all but one of the 'magnet' birds flew more or less straight home, while the homing of those deprived of their sense of smell was badly compromised.[4] A map of the tracks of the anosmic birds (those with their olfactory sense debilitated) is one of aimless wandering over thousands of kilometres, with little sign that they were being drawn back to their breeding sites. Smell, it seems, coupled with the normal mix of the other inputs and memory once in the rough area of 'home', is quite a dominant factor in how the birds get around. Earth's magnetic pull, so vital in the migrations of little songbirds, works rather differently in a shearwater. Having said that, it is really only when homing, as opposed to dispersing, that any disruption of the sense of smell will frustrate the process, so there are many other factors in play at the same time,[5] a key one of which is memory of landmarks once the bird nears a coast.[6]

Seabird navigation, particularly migrational navigation back to the bird's birthplace, is still a hotly debated and much researched branch of science. In a recent paper demonstrating that shearwaters, in the latter days before they fledge, 'imprint onto the magnetic inclination of their natal colony',[7] no fewer than 53 separate papers are cited as references, from as far back as 1958. For the layman, current thinking would simply suggest that the young shearwater goes southwards on the classic 'clock and compass' instincts it is born with, but back north again with, at least partly, the magnetic inclination it developed simply by sitting in a particular location, underground, for the first 70 days of its life. It achieves this by a measurement of the relative steepness of the magnetic field lines that encircle the earth and dip down into the surface, which enables it to recognise latitudes.

Finally, it is easy to overlook one of the most important ingredients in the shearwater's tool-kit for travel, which is that sense of pure restlessness that drives it southwards day after day.

At this point, it starts to get a little bit more scientific, but it's also a demonstration of the brilliance and sheer bloody-mindedness of scientists, once they have got something on their minds. I had always wondered how a bird such as a shearwater, flying huge distances at 30 mph just a few feet above the waves as it does, is able to locate and catch food. After all, it isn't exactly going to detect and be able to react to tiny fish movements 25 feet below the rough surface of the sea. The answer, of course, lies in smell. It turns out from experiments dating all the way back to the 1970s that members of the petrel family, the group that includes shearwaters, have in effect an 'olfactory seascape' available to them, in which the availability of food is announced by increased concentrations of dimethyl sulphide (DMS), which are released into the air at points where krill (the food choice of the shearwater's own food choice) eat the phytoplankton. Put crudely, where a cloud of DMS is discernible, it is highly likely that there will also be food for the shearwater. By flying across the wind until it picks up a stream of DMS, the bird can reliably cover a huge area, and then just zigzag upwind while keeping track of the smell.* Equipped with this inbuilt 'Good Oceanic Food Guide', finding food is rather less hit-and-miss than it might look at first sight.

Maybe 0.01% of all the Manx shearwaters out there are carrying monitoring equipment of one sort or another at any one time, but the combined information that these relatively few birds provide is quite enough to reach a statistically relevant view on how they get around. This allowed me to predict with some degree of assurance roughly where T72 and her friends might eventually pitch up at the other side of the ocean. Or so I thought.

---

* *Bird Sense*, Tim Birkhead (Bloomsbury, 2012). A fascinating sensory account of what it is like to be a bird.

Deep in an old trunk in a forgotten corner of our attic, I eventually found my 1975 O-level Spanish tapes.

It was a language I hadn't spoken in anger, or any other emotion, since an unsuccessful internship at a porcelain business in Valencia a few years after General Franco died, but it was also one in which the entire Argentine birding community exclusively, and not unreasonably, operated, and therefore one with which I was going to have to rapidly re-familiarise myself. As it had been for my army Russian all those years ago, where I never got round to using the one phrase I knew ('I will accept the unconditional surrender of your tank, my friend'), so with Spanish; I just needed to learn loads of seabird terms and I would be fine.

Within a week, I could confidently say: '*Dónde están las pardelas?*'*; to be followed, a minute or so later by: '*Ah! Veo. Ellos tampoco viven aquí.*'† Armed with a few more, mainly food- and drink-related phrases, I grew foolishly confident that I would be able to conduct myself effectively once I left the capital city and wandered my way down the West Atlantic littoral.

Language turned out to be the easiest bit. In order to make a success of the trip, I had first to work out what constituted success which, in turn, meant being very clear with myself about what I wanted from it. If I was entirely honest, I had simply booked the flights the night after I had decided, in principle, to go, so as to stop myself from *not* going. All I knew was that 'following' shearwaters for a year meant, well, actually following them as honestly as I could, which meant being

---

* 'Where are all the shearwaters?'
† 'Ah! I see. They don't live round here either.'

with them in the southern hemisphere for at least part of their summer there.* If I could get myself out to sea for a few days, I would start to build up a genuine picture of how things were for them down there, what other birds were around them, and what problems they faced. However, pelagic birds answer to no fixed itinerary, and there was every chance that I wouldn't see them at all, which argued for a programme of research while I was there among the academics and conservation NGOs of Argentina to ensure the journey was not wasted.

I knew that part of it was, of course, just for the adventure. I was going to Patagonia because 'it was there', and so were the shearwaters. Adventure, after all, flickers intermittently for most of us in middle age, and you need to catch the spark when it comes.

I started to examine online tracking maps that laid out the paths of individual, GPS-equipped adult birds and found, when I looked at a dozen or so overlaid on each other, that the greatest concentrations of activity lay off the coast of a 2,000-mile stretch between Comodoro Rivadavia in the south, and Porto Alegre a little way into Brazil in the north. The second discovery I made was that, for some reason, the birds operated rather closer to the shore than the field guides described, at least they did in the two-year period I was studying, but that anywhere north of Buenos Aires, they appeared to keep well out to sea. For financial and welfare reasons, I wanted to keep my sea trips

....

* I also tried hard to book myself on to a container ship, or banana boat, returning from the Caribbean in January/February but, alas, fear of terrorism has made the operators' insurance companies too nervous to allow it any more.

as short as possible, and so gradually came to the conclusion that I needed to centre my activities in the 400-mile stretch between Mar del Plata in the north and the Valdés Peninsula further south. This was backed up by poring over the results of a major winter tracking exercise from 2006, where the wanderings of twelve birds were successfully recorded, and in which an obvious concentration took place near Valdés for a limited period.[8] What I needed now was a local expert to keep me academically on the straight and narrow.

One name I kept coming across was that of Professor Leandro Tamini of the Albatross Task Force, based at Mar del Plata down the coast from Buenos Aires. Professor Tamini is a leading force in marine conservation, and had recently won a prestigious award[9] for his work on reducing bycatch (fishing fleets accidentally catching and killing the wrong things), which tends to mean seabird deaths from long-line fishing and collisions. This is a major cause of deaths for the wider Procellariiformes order, and it happens when seabirds crash into hawsers, or are attracted to the baited long-line hooks before they have a chance to submerge, get caught up on the barbs and are then drowned as the whole line sinks. Sixty-four seabird species, including the Manx shearwater, have been recorded as dying this way; 23 of them are now threatened with extinction, of which three quarters of the world's albatross species make up the majority.[10] Nowadays, the problem is perhaps less extreme than it was, but then it needs to be: back in 1991, a study showed that around 44,000 albatrosses alone perished each year through being victims of bycatch.[11] It is impossible to put an overall number on the annual deaths but, given that the Alaskan long-line industry alone kills over 20,000 birds, a tenfold multiplication from that doesn't seem an unreasonable exaggeration to get to a figure for the whole world. In an extensive list of factors that have reduced the planet's seabird population by two thirds in the last 60 years, long-line and other fishing is pretty high up on the medal table. To get a better idea of the dangers that T72 and her friends face on a daily basis, the professor would be a great starting point.

He replied to my email straight away, saying that, yes, he would be delighted to give me some time once I got to Mar del Plata a few weeks later. While this was like Beethoven agreeing to help out with some light symphony work, and would almost certainly lead me to other contacts in other places, it didn't sort out the immediate boat problem, which had been further complicated by a contact in Comodoro Rivadavia telling me that the waters off that bit of coast were too rough for small vessel tourism. I could do as many inshore coastal trips as I wanted, but that probably wouldn't find me what I was looking for. Also, I was starting to discover that Patagonia does not enjoy anything like the same vibrant leisure boating industry as we do in the UK, which reduced dramatically the number of boats that would be available to me once I got there. Further north around the Valdés Peninsula, it turned out that November was also peak whale-watching season, and that consequently anyone with a seaworthy boat and a head for numbers would be busy ferrying wealthy Americans a few hundred yards offshore to video large cetaceans nuzzling up to their inflatable. Or at least that is how it seemed.

Mention seabirds to them, and they just laughed.

～⌇～

By mid-October, T72 is flying ever southwards somewhere off the coast of southern Morocco.

When she rises up from the waves and looks out to her left, she will see the dusty African coast lying low on the eastern horizon, ten or twelve miles distant. Across the swell to her right, she can make out the low pyramidal dome of Costa Teguise on Lanzarote in the Canary Islands. These are landmarks that she will come to recognise over the coming years. Ahead of her are other first-year birds flying in the same direction, into which loose grouping she has thrown her lot, and with whom she will raft up on the sea from time to time. This is a Procellariiformes ocean, where eleven types of shearwater converge in different numbers,* and giant petrels of the south will soon replace the puffins, razorbills and guillemots of further north.

There's a simple equation going on here: the more efficiently T72 can fly, the more she reduces her metabolic cost of travel, and thus increases her chances of survival. She is a creature of the winds, and it is only when the wind gets above about 15 knots that she can break out of the flap-glide method of flying that is her stock in trade for short trips, and get into soaring mode, much like a hydrofoil rising up onto its planes as it leaves harbour. When she starts to soar, which she can

....

* Depending on which expert you agree with, there are 19–25 shearwater species worldwide, belonging to three different genera. Together, they cover just about all the world's oceans.

only do down or across the wind, she consumes less energy and therefore needs less food, which will shorten or at least de-complicate her trips. Given that these journeys, especially for young birds like T72, seem to be giant exercises in personal research for the future, and are consequently not just a case of leaving one place and finding the quickest route to another, it is good for her to be efficient. Without those winds she is a much diminished flier, so she will pass as quickly as possible through the calm, so-called horse latitudes between the trade winds and the westerlies that she is now approaching.

Survive, feed, procreate – that's all that will ultimately concern her; and, as she will probably not come back to land for breeding for another four years, her task for now is simply to survive and feed. Although she can travel long distances between meals, she still always needs food. She is not as fussy an eater as many other seabirds, and has a wide-ranging diet that consists of herring, sprat and sardines, complemented by sand eels, small crustaceans and squid. Crucially, at a time when the warming oceans and industrial fishing are playing havoc with individual food chains, as with the more selective puffin, the shearwater's omnivorous menu plan has enabled its numbers to first stabilise, and then rise. For the time being, T72 exists in a world of plenty.

Feeding can be a high-speed activity for a seabird. In a celebrated example back in 2003, a single grey-headed albatross was recorded as *averaging* 127 kph (80 mph) over a nine-hour period between the South Orkneys and South Georgia. On the front edge of a classic Antarctic storm, at one point it was actually flying at over 160 kph, and yet it still had time to stop and feed normally on its journey. While life for T72 is more prosaic, she starts by being instinctively adept at spotting a meal.[12]

She will learn when it is right to feed on the dive down, and when on the ascent to the surface; she will learn that the best fishing will tend to be where the ocean fronts occur, limited areas 'where different bodies of water converge or diverge with shuddering turbulence',[13] and where the planktonic growth that is the bedrock of her food chain will be at its most bountiful. A comprehensive study in 2015[14] demonstrated that older shearwaters gained appreciably more weight per mile of foraging travel than the younger ones, and GPS tracking allowed the researchers to establish that the older ones were doing this by heading straight out to the ocean fronts; in other words, they get better at stuff with experience, just like we do. Although not a natural boat follower, she will learn that certain types of vessel mean disturbance, which means more fishing. And she will learn as the years go by how to interact with rival feeders to ensure that she consistently operates in the best fishing areas. In fact, most of the evidence suggests that T72 will spend the first three to four years of her life simply building up a map of the best places to sustain herself and, at some future time, her own chicks. Education, after all, is not solely a human phenomenon.

Unlike, say, the voracious gannet, whose cruciform shape can be regularly spotted hitting the water from a vertical plunge at 60 miles per hour, she dives quietly down from sitting on the surface. Underwater, she is quick and nimble, using a combination of her feet and wings for propulsion and steering as she chases prey, as adaptable to the element of water as she is unsuited to land. Although she is physiologically able to dive to depths of 70 metres or more, the vast majority of her food is caught somewhere between five and fifteen metres down – making her a relatively shallow diver in comparison to many.[15] On a cloudy day, she will be virtually indistinguishable from the waves as she glides between them, only catching the eye as she rises up a metre or two for the power-gathering phase, when the off-white of her belly might catch the light.

Although T72 will only fully commit to sleep while rafted up on the water, she has the capacity to shut off half her brain while airborne, and to fly slightly higher than normal under the monitoring watch of one half-open eye so long as she is in that state. This allows her to travel prodigious distances without full rest, if need dictates it, and to cover up to 700 or 800 miles in a single 24-hour period. In turn, this frees her up from the normal constraints of day and night, and adds a greater element of efficiency to her migration. Moreover, she can fly in most conditions, though, like the majority of birds, the density of wet air relative to dry air makes her rather less likely to want to fly in heavy rain.[16] She has, after all, spent over 100 million years trying to make life easy for herself.

Briefly, I remembered sitting in front of Michael Brooke at Cambridge three or four months before, and asking him to describe a day in the life of a shearwater, as a way of better understanding how the bird 'worked'.

'A typical day?' He looked a bit taken aback. 'I'm not really sure that it has one.'

The closer I got to the trip, the more the lights of my ordered, routine life faded. I felt myself beckoned towards whatever was out there over the horizon. Because, whatever it was, the best thing about it was that I didn't know and couldn't control it; its very randomness and unpredictability were the things that made it so attractive to me. Somewhere out there were countless acres of the same wilderness that my grandmother's arms had stretched out and pushed me towards all those years before. And in theory, each of those 750,000 square miles of sea had on average only one or two birds in it, so the adventure lay in tracking and finding them. Or not.

On a whim, I went back up to the attic one night and dug around in a suitcase that had a bit of old army stuff in it. There I noticed my old gas-mask, a 1978 military map of Cyprus and a spare set of black uniform buttons; further down I saw a faded photo of my first platoon in Hong Kong, seasoned soldiers who looked like they had just had a twelve-year-old officer dropped onto them; a handful of annual confidential reports ('Captain Morgan-Grenville is a young man in a hurry', said one with foreboding. 'Perhaps too much of a hurry.'). Finally, wrapped in an old piece of khaki material, I found what I was looking for: the 1917 George V penny that my grandmother had sent me while I was in South Georgia. I had carried it around with me just about every day from when she had sent it to me until commercial life got the better of my mystical self when I was around 30. Worn almost blank by the unconscious rubbing of thumb and forefinger while in my right-hand trouser pocket, it had been the small voice in my head reminding me that a journey doesn't necessarily need a destination.

Seasoned travellers, on finding that I was going to Argentina, initially assumed that I was going on the normal round of activities that tourists tended to do in that part of the world: whale watching in the Beagle Channel, seeing the glaciers in Perito Moreno, walking in El Chaltén and drinking more Malbec wine than was good for me in Mendoza.

'And you'll be finishing up at the Iguazú Falls, no doubt?', they might add conspiratorially. 'Good choice.' A couple of hotels were named which, when I looked up the nightly prices, confirmed that they had not been recommended by people who wrote nature books for a living.

'Why aren't you taking Caroline?' one of them asked sensitively, as if my guilty secret would be safe with them once revealed. It was especially tough on her that I wasn't, in fact, as she had been brought up in the country as a young girl and had been longing to go back for around 40 years. Just not necessarily on the cheap, and with no plan beyond trying to get seasick in a few different places and to discuss obscure seabirds with campaigners and academics. She liked nature a great deal, but she probably wasn't quite ready for weeks of travelling around a far continent in acute discomfort with a single-issue fanatic who only wanted to talk about moulting strategies and olfactory bulbs. Staying at home in England would be a small price to pay for avoiding that.

Once I told them that most of my trip would be spent sitting alone on buses with my backpack on my knees, walking up and down pebbly Atlantic beaches trying to persuade local sailors and fishermen to take me out to be with small, half-kilo seabirds somewhere among the oceanic swell on the horizon, their eyes glazed over, and the subject generally changed back to the weather, or the coming election.

Then, early one mid-October morning, I saw from the online tracking reports that at least five early-season Manx shearwaters had been recorded off the Argentine coast by now, which was a clear sign that the older birds, almost certainly including T72's parents, had started to make it down there. The growing number of dots on a faraway map were the first physical proof for me that the miracle journey was real.

———

By reducing as far as I could the degrees of separation between me and the rare boat-owning birders of eastern Argentina, I was gradually getting the outline of a plan together. The British Trust for Ornithology suggested I contact Seabirds.net, a kind of international dating agency for specialist people who want to sit on wet cliffs watching strange birds coming in and out of the mist. They, in turn, produced some people I could contact, even though most of these turned out to be living in the Buenos Aires area and were as far from the ocean physically as they were from being seabird specialists themselves. By painful degrees, I started to build up a list of people down the Atlantic coast who knew one end of a bird from another, which was great, only to find that none of them had boats, which wasn't.

Meanwhile, another complicating factor arose. There being so relatively few birders in Argentina, neither the country nor the wider area can justify an easily obtainable modern and accessible field guide.* And, because a good field guide is the 'get out of jail free' card for every travelling birder, the first and last resort when trying, for example, to distinguish the Cory's and great shearwater from each other, this mattered. Coming from a country in which I could choose from about twelve credible local field guides at any one time, it was also a bit of a surprise.

Finally, I had to decide what kit to bring, which meant balancing the extreme possibility of the local aristocrat asking me in for a convivial evening at his estancia in my dinner jacket with that of me wandering aimlessly around small ports looking for fishermen called Pedro. Pedro and the small port scenario won out, and I opted for an old backpack that was large enough to carry the tools of my trade plus a few clothes, but small enough to allow me to walk a dozen miles or so without relying on anyone else's goodwill if I needed to. Years of getting incrementally more comfortable on holiday gave way to some distant military reflex, and all I knew was that the backpack had weathered the intervening time rather better than its owner. In all, I was only carrying eight kilos, which promised much for efficiency but rather less for hygiene. As always, I needed books, lots of them; and the final one turned out to be a paperback edition of *Asterix in Britain*, for when I got homesick.

As I left for the airport, I had the feeling of being simultaneously as prepared as I possibly could be on the one hand, and utterly reliant on serendipity on the other. Which, while

---

* The best I found was *Birds of Southern South America and Antarctica* (Princeton Illustrated Checklists, 2001). I hope the thief who took it from me in Buenos Aires is enjoying it as much as I would have.

uncomfortable in principle, in practice had an eerie similarity with my entire military career.

—~~—

During the latter part of the night of November 17th, T72 is rafted up somewhere out in the South Atlantic, exactly where we will not know until her geolocator is recovered, with a bit of luck, in about three years' time. The more expensive GPS trackers that had been fitted to a handful of our Skomer birds at the same time have, by now, run out of battery, and are incommunicado. The weather is fine, but under the partial light of a waning moon there is a strong south-easterly wind gusting at 28 to 30 knots and creating waves of two metres.

She is probably aware that most of her journey is done, as the urge to move on has gone. Some of the young birds in whose occasional company she has been flying have been peeling off westwards to the Brazilian coast, and the group is consequently smaller than previously. She does not know that she will fly more or less this exact route, given a bit of luck, for the next 50 years. She does not know that her parents passed this way a fortnight before, and that it is their genetics that will probably determine the specific area in which she will settle for the southern summer. In fact, she will not meet her parents again until she turns up at the burrow of her birth in about three and a half years' time, and wonders why it's not free for her to start a family in.

For the moment, the only being on earth who is interested in her is toying with an inedible cold chicken salad seven miles above the earth, three hours into a fourteen-hour trip towards her.

8. THE MOST EXPENSIVE
BIRD IN THE WORLD

Península Valdés, Argentina

....

If I cease searching, then, woe is me, I am lost.
That is how I look at it – keep going,
keep going, come what may.
VINCENT VAN GOGH, LETTERS

It is proof that, sophisticated man though you
may be, you can still go out with all your worldly
needs on your back and survive in the wild
places. That knowledge is great freedom.
CHRIS BRASHER, *OBSERVER* COLUMN, 2003

....

In the detailed genealogy of my maternal grandparents' line,
my grandmother's birth is recorded as simply 'abroad; possibly 1911', and even that one detail is wrong. She was actually
born in Egypt, and in 1912.

Her father, Ernest, was a prominent architect in a long line of celebrated portraitists, who made his name as Director of Antiquities for the government of Palestine. Art, of one sort or another, flowed richly through the family, as did Catholicism, to which religion he converted in 1926 and which, there being none so passionate as the late convert, dictated the attitudes of much of the rest of his life.

Being a voluntary and lifelong 'displaced person' goes a long way to explaining how my grandmother saw nowhere as home until the closing years of her life on the Ross of Mull. This self-distancing attitude strengthened significantly on April 17th, 1935 when she married a much older, divorced man and her family duly put her into social isolation. The inconvenient fact of her new husband being a multiply decorated First World War airman,* an Air Chief Marshal and, later, leading architect of the air victory in 1940, counted for nothing. He was divorced and was, as far as they were concerned in their high Catholic outrage, sullied goods.†

The ditch between them all became a chasm when, through overwork and stress, he died of a heart attack in 1953, leaving her as a 41-year-old titled widow, with two teenage girls

. . . .

* Air Chief Marshal Sir Wilfrid Freeman GCB, DSO, MC, Knight of the Legion of Honour.

† It was not just Elizabeth who suffered. The royal family, who still at that stage influenced senior positions in the armed forces, and who had no time for divorcees, ensured that Wilfrid's career in the RAF stalled when he was bound towards the top. *Wilfrid Freeman: The Genius Behind Allied Air Supremacy, 1939 to 1945*, Anthony Furse (The History Press, 2000).

and the guiding star of her life gone. Her own war work for the Allied Expeditionary Air Force had led to her receiving an MBE herself in 1945, something that, true to form, we only discovered after she had died and, equally true to form, her own family ignored at the time.

Once her own children had left home, the gravitational pull in her life was always northwards and westwards to the simpler life of an albeit middle-class but hard-grafting crofter, sustained in part by a new set of neighbours who simply didn't have time for social games, and an acre of granite and thin earth that she could make into something. There in her whitewashed cottage above the shores of Loch Caol, she slowly came to terms with the world again, and carved out a meaningful fresh life for herself.

A large part of the new deal was her restless embrace of wilderness, which leached slowly and steadily into the adolescent me. Just at the stage that my more sophisticated contemporaries were going to rock concerts and basically anywhere there was a good crowd, I was trying to find as many ways as possible of getting up to a remote Scottish island. This was partly because it enabled me to avoid the sheer amount of effort involved in being a right-on 1970s teenager, and partly because the mountainscapes and seascapes came over to me in one of the few languages I could understand in my awkward teenage years. Besides, the clouds of smoke from her Abdullah brand full-strength cigarettes more than disguised the occasional Players No. 6 that I would furtively treat myself to in the garden when she wasn't looking. I only tried one of her Abdullahs once, and the coughing fit nearly killed me.

Made manifest by the 1917 penny somewhere in my backpack, she was momentarily on my mind as I blinked into the November sunshine of Buenos Aires and welcomed myself to a new continent.

I could stare at a map or a globe for as long as I liked, but it had taken fourteen hours of watching BA flight 245's glacial progress across the moving map on the screen in front of me to fully comprehend the sheer hugeness of T72's adolescent journey south. Our plane, the same screen told me, was travelling across the ground at nine miles a minute, and yet it needed a full 840 of those minutes to get to Argentina, and it would burn four times my own body weight in oil just to get me there. Even when we crossed the north Brazilian coast at Fortaleza on the equator, we still had five hours' flying to go, 40 more degrees of latitude until we reached the top end of her feeding area. By the time she got there herself, she would be the same latitude south as Tasmania and, allowing for diversions and excursions between feeding and resting, she would probably have racked up 10,000 or 11,000 miles in the weeks since she had left that Skomer burrow. All of this before she was six months old, and without any guidance at all.

Accepting that wildlife and weather answer to no fixed instructions, I had just started to believe that my intricate plan might work. On the basis of exploiting the degrees of separation, where A (a UK academic) knew B (a zoology professor in Brazil), who was friendly with C (a senior director within Aves

Argentina*), who might put me in touch with D (a birder with a boat on the coast), I had gathered a lot of names and numbers. But then it turned out that B was on sabbatical and the chain was broken until I found E (a junior in Aves Argentina), who said he would do his best, but did I also want to meet F (his cousin, a sailor in Comodoro Rivadavia) who knew G (one of the best seabird people in Argentina). And on it went until my name started to be cursed throughout ornithological Latin America, but by which time I had finally been introduced to H (a specialist birder) who had booked a long-distance boat on my behalf with J (a third boat-owner) for an amount of money that I was so embarrassed about I hid it from the entire family. But if that were the price of getting 40 or so miles out, then so be it. H was based in Mar del Plata, 400 miles south of Buenos Aires, but he also had a friend, K, down on the Valdés Peninsula who might be able to take me out to sea in the gaps between coastal whaling trips. I drew the line on the search for connections at the coast: any further inland, and they probably couldn't help. And it was mandatory to my efforts that they knew what a *pardela* was.

In spite of all my intricate plans, it took only an hour or so on Argentine soil to absorb the first of a series of setbacks to my trip.

Before heading down to Patagonia, I had arranged to stay in Buenos Aires for a couple of days to meet with local experts and, almost immediately, I was accidentally and painfully jostled to the floor while passing a small but noisy demonstration

....

* The Argentine RSPB equivalent.

outside a university. Worse was to follow. My day pack was stolen from beside me in a bar close to the Casa Rosada, by means of the oldest trick in the book (a beggar asks for money from your right while his accomplice helps himself to your property on your left as you are refusing). Suddenly, a month's worth of writing notes, my bird books, my itinerary and, saddest of all, the binoculars that my father had given me as a 21st birthday present were all the new property of a presumably disappointed small-time thief in downtown BA. Only the fact that the key valuables were in a money belt around my waist prevented the trip from imploding on Day One, but the setback was serious. To lose four weeks' worth of hand-written research and interviews was enough of a blow, but to lose birding kit that had taken twenty years to accumulate was worse. It couldn't just be replaced on a little shopping trip. Big cities are lonely and frustrating places when you have been thus violated, even when it is mostly your own fault, and I headed off to the hotel to regroup and work out a Plan B. When I sat down on my bed and established Wi-Fi connection, there was a message from H waiting for me, attaching a picture of the weather forecast for the weekend.

'Bad news so far,' he wrote below it. 'There will be storms and little chance of getting to sea. What to do?'

'Plan B?' I emailed back pathetically, hoping he had one. I certainly didn't. Where I came from, Plan B was generally the responsibility of the host.

'No Plan B,' he replied. 'We only see what God will do.'

God, as far as I was concerned, had already expressed himself eloquently through the weather forecasts. Looking at the days of tightly packed isobars on the little weather map on my screen made it appear that he was unlikely to change his mind.

───～───

T72 is out there somewhere on the eastern horizon, largely unaffected by the vagaries of the weather.

By now she has completed her long journey, emulating as she goes the pattern of the winds' highways, and with an inbuilt knowledge of when is the right time to rise up, drop down, shear away or just stop to feed. She is not some automaton, driven by the dictates of an inflexible instinct, but an active decision-maker, an adaptive voyager who can align herself to, or distance herself from, the baseline that is imprinted in her DNA. Just as the captain of BA flight 245 was altering the route based on weather information she was constantly receiving from a computer back in London, so the shearwater decides in real time when to make the big left and right turns and smaller adjustments within her journey. Like that jet, she has time-compensated orientation equipment on board to understand at any time exactly where she is headed.[1] Her destination may be ingrained in instinct, but the changing directions of her voyage towards it are influenced by the availability of food and, above all, the behaviour of the wind.[2] The fact that she is no more than three months old at the start of this journey (possibly the equivalent of six months in a human) is one of the consistent causes of childlike wonder in the scientists I worked with and spoke to.

All in all, the supreme voyager is perfectly equipped for what she has to do.

Although one shearwater species looks much like another, and there are six that regularly ply these southern oceans, identifying the Manxies shouldn't be too difficult. Four of the other five – the great, the sooty, the Cory's and the Cape Verde – are a quarter bigger than the Manx, while the sixth, the little shearwater, is a quarter smaller. Carl Bergmann's controversial rule, to the effect that the colder the weather the larger the body is likely to be, both proves and disproves itself wherever shearwaters go. They are so far-ranging that they defy any attempt to be boxed in by geographical rules. The great shearwater roams, give or take a tiny area, the entire Atlantic; the sooty shearwater's wanderings cover 90% of the world's ocean surface. Restless journeying is the purpose for which the architecture of the bird's body has evolved. Movement, for them, is an entirely natural state.

T72 is already a markedly different bird to the one that took off from the top of that dry-stone wall on Skomer two months ago. She has 10,000 miles of muscle development behind her, for a start, and she has shaken off all the ticks, fleas and mites that had started to torment her in her burrow in the late summer. Her plumage is fresher and blacker than the adults who are now around her, her wings imperceptibly shorter, and she is very slightly smaller than her male contemporaries. Back in the North Atlantic, she will share the rich feeding grounds with the puffins, guillemots, razorbills and auks, but off the coast of Argentina she will be competing with altogether bigger birds – albatrosses, skuas, and the vast, aggressive southern giant petrel. Land has no meaning for her now, other than where its shelving into the sea promises good fishing.

She is not here to breed, to socialise, or to create territories. She is here to feed, to survive and to learn. One of the peculiar gifts that evolution has bestowed on her species is its annual survival rate of 92%, an achievement that has come from doing things slowly, carefully, and – generally – just the once.*

When I arrived a few days later in Mar del Plata, a holiday town a few hundred miles south of Buenos Aires, my first port of call was the ocean's edge. If I thought that things were about to get easier, I was in for a shock. It took only an hour or so for confirmation to come in from Claudio (H) that the skipper he had engaged was not prepared to put to sea on either of the weekend days that we had fixed. It was a blow, even though I had seen it coming for a day or two.

While there should still in theory be shearwaters further south for me the following week, the continental shelf is much narrower towards the north of Argentina, which means birds further inshore, which means shorter sea journeys to find them, and greater concentrations of them when you do. In other words, this part of the trip was supposed to be the banker, with the Valdés bit down south mere pleasure. Once Claudio had made it clear that, with regret, this was the end of the conversation (and conditions at sea over the weekend proved

---

* Compare this statistic with the equivalent for the humble chaffinch (59%) and the European swallow (30%), and you begin to understand the scale of the evolutionary achievement.

him absolutely right) I tried for a while to take matters into my own hands.

I had noticed that Mar del Plata played host to both an Argentine navy detachment and a large deep-sea fishing fleet. Working out for myself that the three naval ships currently in station would possibly have even more compelling things on their agenda than taking a former British army man birdwatching, I set out my stall at the fishing port, having sidled through the security gates while the hired guards weren't looking. Being so obviously not connected with anything going on in the port, people seemed to assume that, whatever I was up to, it was probably more official and more interesting than what they were up to, and they gave me no trouble. I walked along inside the dockyard briskly and quietly, as if I was involved in compliance or health and safety. Deep down, my comfort zone was in another continent, and my pitch sounded lousy. But it was a primarily an adventure, and all good adventures need a healthy element of unplanned activities.

'*Por favor*,' I shouted up at the captain of large red trawler that was gearing up to go out to sea. 'Can I come with you?' I made a vain attempt at a bird flying in sign language. 'I am looking for a bird. *Pardela*.'

The skipper looked as if he felt I should be in an asylum rather than on his boat, lit a cigarette wordlessly and went back into his bridge. After calling up at a couple of what turned out to be unmanned boats, I moved down to the fourth one on the quay, and caught one of the sailors going aboard.

'I would like to go to sea with you,' I said in my best Spanish. I added something about birds. Even as I said it, it sounded all wrong.

'*Por qué?*' he replied, just at the point I realised that a virile young mariner might wonder about the exact motives of this middle-aged man who wanted so badly to go to sea with him. As chat-up lines went, it stank.

'*No es posible.*' He had a point. I would have answered the same way in his position, and probably quite a lot less politely.

And down the line I went. Always the same awkward question, always the same uncompromising answer. Until eventually I got to a small, scruffy trawler, red with rust and with streams of foetid liquid coming out of one of the hawseholes on the deck. The skipper spoke a bit of English, and said that I was welcome to come with him on a two-day trip if that was what I really wanted to do, but it would be rough and they were short-staffed. I'd have to keep out of the way and bring my own food. He was leaving in about two hours.

As I stood on the dock I had one of those moments of deep self-knowledge and honesty. I had promised Caroline that I would not go to sea on anything other than a properly sea-worthy vessel, and I had just signed up for one that looked on its last legs, in a storm, with a crew I had no idea about, and on a trip about which I knew nothing. Having weighed against the possibility of an adventure and seeing Manx shearwaters the distinct possibility of being more seasick than I have ever been in my life, and quite possibly sinking, I walked back to the boat, thanked him profusely, and muttered something about it 'not being important'. It wasn't supposed to be like this.

I returned to my tawdry hotel room, which was becoming like an operations centre with maps, charts and papers lying over the floor and bed. I knew from the GPS tracks roughly where the birds were, and had finally accepted that I had drawn a blank on this section of the trip. No one in Mar del Plata was going to get me out beyond the line of the surf, let alone onto the ocean. I would have to wait for Valdés the following week. One of the guides I was in contact with down there was confident that he could find the birds for me.

'I like a challenge,' he had signed off his last email, adding with great honesty that he quite liked the idea of the US dollars, as well.

Statistically, I was in tricky territory. For a start, there was the search area of 750,000 square miles (or eight times the size of Great Britain) to locate the birds. But it was only when I read one of Leo Tamini's academic papers that the scale of the challenge really manifested itself.[3] There in the appendix, in a list of 23 seabirds that had been observed around trawlers during 367 censuses over 480 hauls and seven years' work, Manx shearwaters had only been seen on 0.3% of the interactions. As some annoying person in my previous life used never to tire of saying: 'Do the math.' 0.3% of 480 effectively meant 'once'. It might have been useful if I had read this particular paper before leaving home in the first place.

I had to admit that this whole trip had looked a lot more effective in theory back at my desk in Sussex than it did in practice on the ground. Right now I was allowing myself to be blown around by circumstances, rather than making things happen and cutting the vaguely heroic figure that I had had in mind before I left home.

As I packed my kit for the following day's flight to Patagonia, something small and metallic fell out of one of the side pockets of my rucksack onto the tile floor. It was my grand-mother's old penny, and it was the first time I had seen it since packing over a week ago. Holding it, I wondered momentarily what she would do or say at a time like this.

'Press on regardless,' is what she would say. It's what she always said. She said it whether she was doing a mad piece of overtaking, weeding her carrots or placing a bet down the tele-phone with her bookmaker. I smiled at the thought that each of her grandchildren would have come up with the same answer if asked the same question.

Anyway, it was time to go and meet Leo.

Down on a southern ocean, T72 probably has a great deal less to fear than in the days leading up to her fledging. The occasional seabird sitting on the water will become a welcome change of diet for a large fish, but otherwise it is only extreme weather, and man, who interpose. Man in the form of our spe-cies' insatiable desire for fish, and the way that the industry goes out and catches it.

I met Leo Tamini and his colleague, Leandro Nahuel Chavez, in a quiet beachside bar to discuss the work of the Albatross Task Force, an organisation dedicated to reducing unnecessary deaths in pelagic seabirds, a cornerstone cause of the two-thirds decline in seabird numbers since 1960.[4] Both have spent over two decades of their lives on this crusade, alternating between desk research and 30- or 40-day sea trips in the rough southern oceans monitoring bycatch from the fishing vessels themselves. It was yet another example to me of unsung science trying to protect us from ourselves.

'When I get home after a trip,' Leandro smiles, 'I smell so bad my wife doesn't know whether to laugh or cry.'

To a seabird, a boat normally means food. This could be in the form of discarded offal, bait or disturbed and trapped fish, but it is why trawlers become bird magnets. The numbers are staggering, with up to 500 albatrosses, petrels and shearwaters fighting for food in the immediate area of the back of the boat; indeed, it would be one of nature's great sights were it not for the attendant lethal dangers. Most birds survive the experience, but a sizeable proportion become avoidable casualties, either through getting hooked on the baited long-lines or colliding with the strong wires that hold the nets. Mitigating techniques have been developed, like fast-sinking lines and bird-scaring streamers, and the evidence is that they perform extraordinarily well if the patchily regulated fishing industry actually bothers to adopt them. With such a great reduction in the biomass of the world's seabirds over the last 60 years, this is a problem that can only end one way if ignored.

To an extent, T72 is lucky. Manx shearwaters are not ship followers, by and large, and they tend to dive too deep, anyway, to be much affected by the surface actions of nets and lines. Unlike the albatross, with its enormous wings which are extended when it feeds, the shearwater is a plunge diver, and a relatively small one to boot. So, while the foraging divers, like penguins, may get caught in the nets deep down, and the surface feeders, like albatrosses, get injured around the trawler, evolution has granted the shearwaters something of a free pass

in their space in the middle depths. But T72 is also an opportunist at heart, and will attend a feeding frenzy with the same
enthusiasm as any other bird if she happens upon it. And the
biggest problem for an opportunist shearwater is getting stuck
in the net when it is pulled back into the boat; Leo showed me a
picture of four lifeless great shearwaters that had been retrieved
from just one net a couple of years ago.

'Very beautiful,' he sighed. 'But more beautiful when flying.'

I asked him if he felt it was a battle that he was winning.

'Sometimes,' he said. 'Sometimes, when one of us has been
on a trawler for four or five weeks, maybe a couple of members
of the crew understand that what we are doing is important.
It is a cultural thing,' he added, mentioning a list of countries
that minded, and those that didn't seem to.

Necessity, as we all know from the copybooks of our
schooldays, is the mother of invention, and Leo's work is now
even being aided by the albatrosses themselves. Based on the
fact that the birds are large, far-ranging and attracted to fishing
boats from a distance of fifteen miles out, a group of scientists have successfully experimented with attaching loggers
onto their backs which, on the one hand, register that there
is a fishing boat there from its active radar signal and, on the
other, can work out if it has illegally switched off its Automatic
Identification System (AIS), and then relay the information
back via satellite in real time. In the six-month trial ending in
June 2019, it was established that almost 30% of the contact
boats thus unwittingly observed by the albatrosses were fishing illegally.[5]

But in a way, the problem is much more straightforward

than it first looks. Seven billion humans simply want to eat more seafood than the oceans can comfortably provide us with. Depending on whose statistics you absorb, we catch and eat somewhere between 1 and 2.7 trillion fish each year, or 80 million tons,[6] and over 90% of the world's fish stocks are either fully or over-exploited.[7] That catch is currently ten times the eight million tons of plastic that we dump into the ocean to replace it with,[8] but it won't be for long. It doesn't help that 23% of what we catch out in those deep seas is fed straight back to farmed fish nearer to land,[9] which then become potential sources of infection to the wild inshore fish. Conservationists like Leo will continue to work, innovate, cajole and hope, scoring the occasional notable victory, but their efforts are fated to be a drop in the oceans they work so hard to protect until the industry, and its end consumers, take it far more seriously. And that seriousness starts with taking a sharp interest in how, and under what conditions, the fish they are thinking of buying has been caught.

As in so many parts of our complex lives, until we are satisfied with less, the whole oceanic food chain will pay the price. The whole planet, in fact.

~

When I eventually reached the far point of my journey a week later at Puerto Pirámides, an old salt-mining settlement on the isthmus onto the deserted Valdés Peninsula, my reputation, such as it had had time to evolve in the two weeks that I had been in the country, had preceded me.

'Ah! The *pardela* man,' said the owner of the hostel, cheerfully, when I checked in. He looked as though it was all really quite funny, which, if you weren't me, it was. I noticed that he took payment in full before he allowed me into my room, which he certainly hadn't done for the pair of students who checked in just in front of me. When I checked the vacant face with the wild hair in the bathroom mirror once I had finally accessed the room, I could see that his precautionary move had been entirely reasonable. I would have done the same.

The strong wind that had plagued me in Mar del Plata was once again conspiring to keep boats ashore further south, and a trip to the distant mouth of the Golfo Nuevo was for the time being out of the question.

So for a few days I lost myself in the harsh beauty of the Patagonian coastal wilderness, and it became increasingly pointless to mar the adventure with the frustration of not seeing a Manx shearwater. This was, indeed, the world 'beyond the pavement' that I had always been seeking, a vast domain of rock and salt and scrub, surrounded and given life by the relentless Atlantic. Famous for its beaching orcas and vast seal colonies, it demanded instead from me a complete deceleration in the pace of my life, to the point at which I would just sit myself down on any old headland with a bottle of water, a sandwich and my new binoculars and wait for the wildlife to come to me. Which it did: eagles, vultures, sea lions, and mother-and-calf right whales in profusion in the white-flecked bays below. Sure, I continued to look out to sea for my birds for days on end from headland to rocky headland, but I had begun to find other reasons to come here as well.

'Go and see the huge penguin colony at San Lorenzo,' said the man at the hostel. 'Only US$40. Many, many penguins. Maybe one hour drive.'

I could hardly tell him that I had spent months of my life being paid by my government to be on one of the most important penguin islands on the planet, as it was an island still beyond any polite conversation in Argentina.* I had quickly discovered through posters, graffiti, murals, car stickers and leaflets that memories live long and hard along the bleach-white shoreline of Patagonia and that, although the Falklands war had been fought 37 years ago, it was as good as yesterday on this coast. Out here, the destiny of the Islas Malvinas was a live issue far beyond just respect for the 649 Argentine servicemen who died in the battle. More than memory, and paradoxically in a country with strong British affections and ties, the issue of the Malvinas was practically a shadow religion down in Patagonia.

At breakfast on the penultimate day of my stay, my host asked me what I would be doing. I told him I would be writing. It seemed very much as if the ceaseless wind was going to have the last word on my search.

'Boats OK again this evening, and tomorrow,' he said. 'Better go to Punta Pardelas this morning.'

I laughed thinly at this gentle poke at my odyssey. As far as I knew, there was no such place as 'Shearwater Point', and he was just being funny. In order to catch my flight up to Buenos Aires, I had to be out of the village by 11.30 the following

....

* A surprising footnote to all this is that around 25% of the world's penguins currently live on British territory (RSPB tweet, 2018).

morning, and was fast running out of time. Indeed, I had already reached an accord with myself about failing to see a single Manx shearwater during my trip.

'*Si*!', he came back strongly, and pointed down the beach. 'Serious. Look at the map. Maybe two, three hours to walk there. No road. But,' and he smiled anew, 'maybe *pardelas*!' He had fully entered into the spirit of my search, as had half his friends, and he articulated the word '*pardelas*' as if it were some religious incantation. These were sea people, good people, and they wanted to help.

There were no detailed maps of the Valdés Peninsula available, but when I got back to my room and looked it up online, I found that Pardela Point was a thing, a real thing. 'It is the best place in Argentina to observe these pelagic birds from land', said the literature of the reserve. I had no idea. Granted, they would probably be sooty shearwaters, not the smaller, lighter Manxies, but they would be a start. Equally, I had seen all the many Oxnav tracking information maps and graphs, and there was absolutely no question that my birds also regularly transited the Golfo Nuevo, whatever the locals said. Shearwaters mix together in different breeds, so there was at least a chance; and besides, the one dividend of the onshore winds should be the ocean-going birds coming inshore for calmer fishing. T72 it might not be, but we were getting warmer.

Not wasting any time working out how I could have been so stupid as to have missed the place during all my research, I threw a few cold water bottles into my rucksack and headed off down the beach into the blinding sunshine. An hour later, where the coast turned sharply southwards, the beach ran out and I had to scale a low line of shell-laden cliffs to get to the higher ground. From there, it was just a question of heading south through the thorn scrub for another hour until I got to the general vicinity of the headland. This was a new-minted world of aloof guanacos, pumas, hares and caracaras, a place where the only sounds were the crash of the surf far below and the mew of the kelp gulls above. Eventually, the ground started tilting downwards until I could see the landmark island in front of me, and knew that I was at Punta Pardelas. In a journey without specific destinations, the very name marked this out as being a station of the cross towards the end of my quiet pilgrimage.

I found a spot in the shade of a large rock and scanned the sea below, watching the stiff-winged giant petrels and royal cormorants. For a second or two, I found myself half marvelling and half chuckling about what had happened to my life. I was where I had always wanted to be, far away and below a sky full of birds. This was the wilderness that I had been seeking, a place beyond both help, if I got into trouble, and interruption, if I didn't. This was what being close to nature had eventually become for me; not nature as in just a search for 'primroses and otters',* but nature as in being immersed in anything that is not man-made, nature in the sense of everything around me. Shearwater or no shearwater, I knew that this was the possible completing of a gigantic circle that had taken me 8,000 miles from home. I watched the rhythm of the boundless ocean, breath by tidal breath, for an hour or two, maybe three.

....

* From *Sightlines*, Kathleen Jamie (Sort of Books, 2012).

Flap, flap, flap, glide. Only one bird that size and shape does that. I snatched up the binoculars and focused them in on a dark bird two or three hundred yards away. Flap, flap, flap, glide. How many times had I seen that up in the Hebrides and out in the Welsh islands during the summer? Flap, flap, flap, glide, shearing the waves southwards in insolent defiance of the notion that shearwaters are only seen from ships far out to sea.

It was a shearwater. After a week of crumpled effort, I had finally found a shearwater where I had least expected to, from a rock on the shore. A sooty shearwater, maybe, but a shearwater nonetheless. Tiny speck on the vast Patagonian coast that I may have been, I punched the air as if I'd just scored the winning goal of the FA Cup final, and there is nothing quite so pathetic as a grown man punching the air five miles from the nearest human being. As much as anything, I was delighted for my hostel landlord.

And I was closing in.

Flap, flap, flap, glide.

It was nine o'clock the following morning, my last day in Patagonia.

The previous night, I had been explaining about T72 to a group of student volunteers and backpackers in a bar, when they had asked me what I was doing in Puerto Pirámides.

'I can be very boring about birds, so please stop me,' I said, because I can; but they hadn't, as it turned out that we all could. We all drank far too much cheap beer as we explained to each other the little ambitions, chances and accidents that had brought us to this place to do these things. Slowly, the feeling that I was an awkward interloper in the party of a generation who had their own dreams gave way: this was simply a confederation of like-minded people who just wanted to tell conservation stories and get stuff done to protect the things they loved. Whoever we were, and however we had done it, we had all thrown off the chains that bound us to an endless acceptance of 'the way things were'.

'How old is your father?' I asked Rodrigo as we lurched back down the hill to the village.

'Forty-eight,' he replied. 'And it makes me sad that he will never give himself the chance to do what you are doing now.' Unsuccessfully suppressing a belch, he told me that I was simultaneously ten years older than his father, and twenty years younger.

'You are so lucky,' he added, with feeling.

It had taken seven days of trying, and for the second time in fourteen hours, I was finally out at sea. The previous evening's trip had produced whales, dolphins and sea lions in great multitudes, but no more shearwaters. By mid-afternoon I would be six miles up and starting the long journey home, but for now I was sitting on the edge of a whale-watching boat, observing 37 people staring at nature not in its full glory, but via the screens of their mobile phones, the peaceful beauty of a 40-ton right whale and her calf fated not to be a precious memory but a series of substandard images on a playlist. Determined not to ruin any memory of the whales for myself, I had left the camera back on dry land, and my phone deep at the bottom of my rucksack. More than anything, this was about the memory. Besides, I could count in the thousands the sub-standard photos that I had taken over the years of amazing wildlife events.

'No photos?', asked one of the guides.

'No photos,' I confirmed. I told him also that I was more interested in the birds.

Behind us was the startling bare whiteness of the rocky shoreline, rolling on inexorably into the distance.

'Ah! Penguin!', he said in delight, pointing at two small shapes swimming along just off the starboard side of the boat. 'There's a bird for you.' As with the puffin up north, so with the penguin down here: always top of the list of birds that people want to see.

That's when I saw it, out beyond the penguins.

Out in the open sea, almost too far to see without binoculars, was that familiar 'flap, flap, flap, glide'. Then another, and a third. They were lighter and smaller than the sooty shearwaters I had seen yesterday, and by some degree bigger than if they had been the delicate little shearwater. Swiftly, by a process of elimination, I worked out that the only birds they could be were Manx shearwaters. Barely a mile off shore, and well within the bay area where locals insisted they never went, I had finally found what I came all this way to look for. There again was that sense of bustle and purpose, that rising just above the wave tops before dropping back down behind them, straight-winged and graceful. Here were the familiar patterns of flight that I had seen off Skomer, Rum and Mull, here in the last place I could try and, frankly, the last place that I would have looked. Just to have travelled the same road behind them, and to have found them, made me let out something that may even have been an involuntary cheer.

'They're good,' said the guide, sensing my enthusiasm, but attributing it to the wrong bird. 'Magellanic penguins. You like?'

'Yup,' I lied. 'I like them.'

I had kept my promise and had come to their oceans. For their part, they had made no promises, but they happened to have come to me all the same. My heart skipped a beat or two as they darted over the seaward waves a hundred yards away.

Like momentarily glimpsing the Mona Lisa from afar over the heads of a crowded gallery, I had finally found what I had come for, not in the way that I had imagined, but honestly, nonetheless. Sometimes, I knew, you just have to see things with your own eyes.

'*Pardelas*!' said the guide, noticing what I was looking at. 'Not as exciting as the penguins, I think.'

I watched the tiny group shearing away from me across the waves, much as I had watched them in the Sound of Rum five months ago, small familiar darts of sleek dark-white movement over the face of the endless sea, and I knew, without argument or regret, that, wherever she was, I would never see T72 again. But then I had known that all along.

In time, she will head northwards to complete her adolescence in the summer seas somewhere, maybe off Venezuela, maybe Cuba. She, like all young shearwaters, is a creature of discovery as much as habit, and she won't necessarily go back to the same southern summer place a second time. If she is reasonably lucky, she will survive into adulthood. She will learn from the other birds, from the ocean, and from herself, and in time she will bring all that experience back with her to Skomer, where she will search for a mate and a burrow and establish a new lineage.

I will move on, too. In the blink of an eye my shearwater year will be gone, and whatever happens in burrow number T72, it will eventually no longer be my business, and rightly so. 'They are birds, not people,' my grandmother would have said to me.

She was right, of course, but I had been in this far too deep, and for far too long, to believe it for one second.

Part Two

HOMEWARD
BOUND

9. A CABLE CAR AND
A HOMECOMING

March, West Cork, Ireland

....

Magnetic meridians, coast lines and river channels;
food supply and sex impulses; hunger and love,
homing instincts and inherited or acquired memory,
thermometer, barometer and hygrometer, may all be
factors in the problem. But none of them, and not all
such together, can completely satisfy the whole equation.
CHARLES DIXON

Nullius in verba (Take no one's word for it)
MOTTO OF THE ROYAL SOCIETY
....

It was a winter of named storms and of approaching panic.
From the bushfires of New South Wales to submerged
villages in Yorkshire, from the locust swarms of East Africa to
the little crown-shaped virus seeping its explosive path across

the world from Wuhan, there was a sense that, for humans at any rate, life had suddenly become much more complex and rather less in our gift to control. Elegant and long-laid plans fell to the ground like autumn leaves, mine included.

Every morning, though, I still awoke with the simple thought that the shearwaters were bearing down across the wild Atlantic Ocean and heading for home. Sometime after the New Year, a deep restlessness, driven by the need to reproduce, would have stirred within them, the first sign of the coming journey back to their colonies. That restlessness, or *zugunruhe** to give it its more precise name, actually arises from two different rhythms coinciding within their body clock: circadian (based on the earth's daily rotation, and broadly affecting bodily changes, such as temperature and alertness) and circannual (based on the annual cycle of the earth, and governing changes in behaviour). It is this way for all migrating birds, and genetically wired in to how they will live their lives.[1]

Whereas on the way down, the shearwaters had broadly headed southwards along the European and African western coasts, to take advantage of the wind systems, on the way back they will keep close to the American landmass, so that eventually the clockwise North Atlantic gyre will bring them home. Counterintuitively, for a bird that should be flying northeastwards towards Europe, a returning shearwater in fact turns sharply to the west when it reaches the top 'corner' of South America, and flies off into the Caribbean Sea. As we already know, they go down on the right, and back on the left. Indeed,

----

* From the German *Zug* (move) and *Unruhe* (anxiety).

if you overlay the routes of any number of tracked birds (see Map 2) you will be left with a million square miles of mid-Atlantic where they scarcely ever go. And by the time they turn towards the British Isles, they are already at the latitude of Florida, or Chesapeake Bay, or Newfoundland, at least 6,000 miles away from Argentina. The more adventurous of them will see the lights of Miami long before they see Milford Haven or Mallaig. Since the Manx shearwater was first noticed breeding in Massachusetts in 1973, and then in Newfoundland in 1976, they have become much less of a rarity on the west side of the North Atlantic, and it is generally suspected that they are now nesting on the Pacific coasts of Alaska and British Columbia as well.

They fly together and yet they fly alone. Drawn variously by that cocktail of magnetic force, smell, sun, stars and memory, they live well, and probably feed often. I say 'probably' as this is the part of their journey least known to science, out of battery range for GPS* and furthest away from the attentions of last summer's scientists. Sleeping on the water, or half-sleeping in the air, all we really know is that they are drawn home by nature's most powerful imperative of creating offspring. With their life expectancy of up to 50 years, T72 may be the middle child of 20, or even 30, in a long marriage. But we already know that we have seen the last of her, out there on her adolescence in the Americas. Until she returns to breed, she will always be far from land.

....

* Ironically, battery technology appears to be improving at a slower speed than tracking technology, and our struggles to perfect lithium (and even graphene) batteries have helped to extend birds' private moments just a little.

Poring over a very old book on Irish lighthouse observations in the warmth of the Radcliffe Science Library in Oxford on a soggy December afternoon, I started to get an idea of the most likely places to catch the shearwaters making landfall after their journey home. And, although the answer was 'just about any south-westerly-facing headland in the bottom left-hand corner of the country', my thirst for variety was nudging me in the direction of Blannan headland on Ireland's southernmost inhabited land, Cape Clear Island. Look at a map of the Atlantic, and you cannot fail to notice the four fingers of land pointing out from the south-western tip of Ireland, and cannot fail to appreciate why so many migratory birds make their landfall there. There are small breeding colonies of Manxies dotted all the way up the coasts of Counties Kerry, Galway and Mayo, but none down south in County Cork, meaning that those I would see from there were likely to be Welsh birds routing home, which were the ones I wanted to see. The first outliers might be passing by in early February, and there should be something of a stream of them by the end of the month. They would probably be following much of the same route that Lockley and Matthews' celebrated bird flew between June 3rd and June 16th, 1952, after it had been taken to Boston among the luggage of a Skokholm visitor, and unceremoniously released on Logan Airport's perimeter around about lunchtime. Orientating itself immediately, the bird headed eastwards to the ocean and was back in its burrow 3,000 miles away twelve days later.

Short of putting myself in a boat a thousand miles out into the Atlantic Ocean, this was about as faithfully as I could keep my promise to follow them through their year. Science had unlocked all the shearwater secrets that I had learned in the last year, but there was nothing science could do to get me closer now.

~

If sex began in 1963,* and science began way back in 1660 with the formation of the Royal Society, the heyday of the study of birds had to wait until the blossoming of the Victorian gentleman naturalist. Men like ornithologist Charles Dixon who, at the age of 34, was already very sure of himself, cocky even.

'We can afford to put aside', he wrote dismissively in his 1892 book on bird migration, 'Middendorf's suggestion that the bird is impelled or dragged by magnetic force.'[2] Much of what he went on to write was wild guesswork, possibly sustained by the fact that he was also a creationist, but on this point regarding the shearwater, he ended up being just about right. Inspired guesswork featured highly in the toolbox of late-Victorian natural historians, and the extraordinary thing is not how much they got wrong in the absence of the technical help we have today, but just how much they got right. Looking through the old books, however, you get a feeling that each author started from a strong, often anti-Darwinian standpoint, and then built each bird around a mixture of their observation and their beliefs, rather than the science. 'They are somewhat addicted to twilight, flying abroad when the stars glimmer red, to take their pastime and seek their daily food,' wrote the Reverend F.O. Morris of

....

* Well, at least according to Philip Larkin, it did.

the shearwater, with a charming turn of phrase in his *Morris's British Birds*, and 'are said to be much attached to their young.'*

Scientific books back then were in good part given over to the rubbishing of other scientists' work, particularly if the scientist concerned was foreign, but once that important task had been taken care of, they could get down to the business of recording the observations, analysis and occasional pure guesswork of the gentleman biologist. Sometimes they got it completely wrong ('The Manx shearwater is resident with us throughout the year ...'†). Even then, and given the difficulty of knowing what happened beyond the limit of their eyesight, they knew rather more than you might think.

They knew, for example, that any western Holarctic‡ bird generally wanted to breed in the coldest (i.e. northernmost) part of its range, and that they had first been driven southwards for the northern winter by global cooling. They knew about moulting patterns, and the conditions needed before a long journey; they knew about weather delays and shortest

....

* F.O. Morris (1810–93) was an irascible Irish clergyman and author who, on the one hand, was an early father of conservation while, on the other, raiding birds' nests at will. His place in history is secured by the beautiful books he wrote, and by his part in bringing the plumage industry to an end.

† *The Birds of Britain*, J. Lewis Bonhote (1907). I love that his 1922 obituary goes on to say: 'he would often take on a view he knew to be erroneous for sheer love of arguing from the opposite side.' Not quite what I remember my own science lessons advocating.

‡ The Holarctic region, in bird-watching terms, is a 2,000-mile-wide belt around the northern hemisphere approximately coinciding with the latitudes of Europe.

possible sea crossings; about the birds' natural attraction to light ('fiery points of attraction'), and about the three perils ('fatigue, natural enemies and blunders'). They knew about relative heights flown and about the wing structures of migratory birds; and about the role of adult birds in the training of the younger ones. And they understood the concept of climate change ('the slow progression of the equinoxes, and the increasing eccentricities of the earth in orbit') such as it was, 70 years before it even became a general point of discussion. From Irish lighthouses and lightships, their work on seabirds was corroborated or disproved by the meticulous observations of anything that flew past, over, under, or into their workplaces, day and night, winter and summer: '35 mackerel cocks [shearwaters] reported as striking the lighthouse. Nocturnal habits do not prevent occasional bewilderment at night'[3] – a truth to which any undergraduate will testify. They were even releasing sooty terns in blind orientation exercises off the Florida coast 40 years before Lockley ever had the notion to do so with shearwaters from his Skokholm cottage. All in all, they knew a lot, and not much of where they went amiss was proved to be so until our own century.

But on two specific things regarding the Manx shearwater, Dixon and his competitors were completely wrong: they discounted the influence of smell from the bird's migratory menu; and they reckoned the shearwaters went west to the Caribbean and the eastern United States for their wintering, rather than south to the Atlantic coast of Argentina. After all, that was the direction from which the Irish lighthouses recorded them returning at the beginning of the breeding season, and it was not an idiocy to assume that they were coming in from where they had been living out those months.

Given that they operated before scientific ringing,* let alone GPS, these errors were understandable. Two world wars then ensured that bird science largely marked time for the first half of the twentieth century, and it wasn't until 1952 that the ringed corpse found on a Brazilian beach suggested that their original guess had been about 5,000 miles out. It was to be more than another half a century before they started to discover where the youngest Manx shearwaters went once they had left their fishing grounds at the end of the southern summer.

When I asked Tim Guilford, in an unguarded moment, what he reckoned were the keystone moments in the development of seabird science, his first reaction was to ask me exactly what I meant, so that, as a scientist, he didn't run the risk of answering a question I hadn't actually asked. Once he understood that it was just an opinion I wanted, and not detailed research, his eyes sparkled with the joy and enthusiasm of someone who has never once in 35 years tired of his day job.

'Two things,' he said. 'Niko Tinbergen's work on herring gulls in the middle of last century, which really paved the way for all the animal behaviour study that has gone on ever since, including everything that I have done and worked on.† And then the development of tracking devices which have, only very

---

* The first recorded ringing for scientific purposes, rather than for sending messages or showing ownership, was done with starlings by Hans Christian Mortensen, a Danish schoolteacher, in 1899.

† Niko Tinbergen (1907–88) was a Dutch scientist who made the link between visual cues (e.g. the red dot on a herring gull's bill) and the

recently, allowed us to follow these birds when they go beyond the horizon.'

Those shearwaters that were even now flying back across the North Atlantic had previously been a riddle wrapped in a mystery inside an enigma, to steal a phrase from Churchill. These days, we know not only that they are on their way, but from what direction and with exactly what navigational inputs. If we want to know, we can even tell what they have eaten, when they ate it, and how deep they went down for it.

Bit by bit, we have successfully intruded on their most private moments.

On my first full day in Ireland, I had set the alarm early to catch the shipping forecast, as the crew of the little ferry boat had warned me that any swell above four metres would effectively kill off any chance of landing me on Cape Clear. What I heard on the radio on Sunday morning would be the key influence on what the sea state would be like on Monday, the day I was trying to get over.

'There are warnings of gales,' said the disembodied voice rather too cheerfully for my liking, 'in Sole, Lundy, Fastnet and Irish Sea.' I sat up in bed and listened for the general synopsis ('Low Bailey 972 expected Hebrides by midnight'), and then the all-important area forecasts for the next 24 hours: 'Lundy,

....

behaviour of the chick trying to get a meal from its parents. Joint recipient of the 1973 Nobel Prize for Physiology and Medicine.

Fastnet, Irish Sea. South-west veering west 5–7, gale 8, occasionally severe gale 9 later. Showers; good; occasionally moderate.' South-west we could deal with, as the harbour was on the north of the island, but severe gale 9 was another issue altogether.

Suddenly bed seemed a rather good place to remain, the polar opposite of being on a tiny boat heading out of Baltimore Harbour some five miles away. Because then there was also the promise of inches of rain: at least that hadn't been an issue down south. Having thought that I had left the annoying wind gods safely behind in Patagonia, I now understood that they had followed me back not just to Europe, but to my very post-code, and were even now rifling through my diary to see where I was headed next. 'There would probably', I thought to myself, 'have been easier years than this to chase a seabird.'

A few hours later, I was sitting in a bar in the village, having duly confirmed that the ferry could not and would not be putting to sea tomorrow or the next day. If there had been a Plan B, now would have been the time for it; in fact, if there had even been a Plan A2, it might have helped. The talk when I entered the bar was of the venomous enthusiasm with which the local Garda chief was enforcing the drink-drive rules to the detriment of civilised social gathering, but it soon turned gently to me, and to what I might be doing in the area. I explained that the birds I was studying would pass close to the Irish coast on their way back to Wales, and that all I wanted to do was clap eyes on them for a bit.

'Ah, seabirds, you say?' said the barman, and off it all kicked. Everyone in the bar had a confident opinion as to where the shearwaters were to be found, irrespective of whether they had actually heard of the bird, and every opinion was different. In the interests of hospitality, inland ponds were suggested, as were local streams and even a flooded football pitch just on the edge of nearby Skibbereen. Eventually someone suggested Dermot, who was duly dragged out of a back room and who had, indeed, heard of the Manx shearwater.

'He'll tell you!' said the barman, brandishing Dermot as if he were a conjuring trick. 'He's something of a birder.'

Dermot eyed me up and down and eventually came to the apparent conclusion that I, too, was something of a birder.

'Well, if you can't get to Cape, then you'll need to go to the Beacon.' My not knowing where the Beacon might be was brushed off with a mere flick of the arm southwards across the rainy harbour. When I demurred, he got a grubby envelope and blunt crayon out of his back pocket and drew a hieroglyphic headland to the delight of the rest of the audience.

'That'll be your best bet,' agreed one of the early drinkers, suddenly an expert as well. 'There's loads of them down there.'

'And if I don't see any there?'

'Ah, then,' said Dermot to the evident enthusiasm of the others, 'then, you'll need to go to Mizen Head.' This recommendation found general agreement, and the prevailing sentiment was that Mizen Head would, indeed, be a good place to go.

'Like he says,' said a fresh voice. 'Mizen Head will be perfect.' The consensus among the ten or so drinkers was that Dermot was doing the village proud.

'Which is where?'

'Over there,' and the hand swept westwards over a distant headland, and more ink smudged on to the envelope. 'An hour away.' And bit by bit, the envelope filled with overlapping maps of headlands and strange names, and the crowd around us grew with the good people of Baltimore who, just like the good people of Puerto Pirámides a few months before, clearly and genuinely wanted me to find what I had come to their home looking for. Apart from anything, they had the grace not to treat me as some single-issue obsessive as others had; indeed, as I sometimes did myself.

'Start at the Beacon,' said Dermot as I left him at the bar, nursing a fresh and precautionary pint that I had lined up for him. He cheerfully waved his hand towards due north, 180 degrees from where he had pointed last time he had mentioned it.

If I thought following early-season Manx shearwaters was going to be any easier than it had been in Argentina three months earlier, the winter of successive named storms had soon put me right. However, it is an ill wind that blows nobody any good, and the very winds that were preventing people like me getting out to the islands, were blowing T72's parents across 3,500 miles of ocean in double-quick time. Shearwaters may well be able to cross the bulk of the Atlantic in no more than a week, and still have time for a couple of good fish suppers.

Now that T72 was learning her trade for the coming summers over sunnier seas, I had decided to follow, notionally at least, her parents who, in all probability, would pair up again and occupy the same 'study burrow' as the previous year. If nothing else, it was an approach that prevented it all from being too abstract.

Her father, T72M, will generally arrive a couple of weeks earlier than his partner, whom he almost certainly hasn't seen since September. He has, as we shall see, much work to do back on Skomer, and landfall in the European continent will be somewhere around these shores. Shearing his way more downwind than across it, he can already sense from the shallowing and breaking seas, the coastal gulls, the gannets, the cormorants, the rocks and fishing boats that he is nearing his journey's end. Up to this point, he has been driven by smell and by magnetic fields only, as the prevailing Atlantic conditions have ruled out any reliable dependence on the sun and stars. When he reaches landfall off the southern Irish coast, visual memory will at least partially take over, and he will from now on also be guided by the subtle language of cliffs, rocks, channels and bays that make up the remainder of his 200-mile journey back to Skomer. It is likely that he will return this way more than once in the coming summer for his major foraging expeditions out into the Atlantic, so he will come to know the coast well. If he doesn't stop to fish, he could be back on the fringes of his island in a mere five or six hours from now.

In the time that I have been in that bar with Dermot, he has bustled his way through the salty air a few feet above the water for maybe 40 miles. He is sleek and healthy, having fed well among the turbulences of the North Atlantic Ridge, and it is just as well, as he is entering by far the tougher half of his year. Soon, he will need all the conditioning on him that he can manage.

T72M is but one shearwater in a vast re-gathering of oceanic seabirds on the coastal cliffs and islands of Britain, a diaspora in reverse that makes a marked difference to the avian biomass* of our region. Imagine, for a second, that every oceanic bird that breeds here had a GPS strapped to the ring on its leg, and was contributing to a vast real-time moving map of lines, with a different colour for each species. On any given early March day, there would be a huge web of approaching coloured lines: blue shearwater lines coming in eastwards past Ireland, a concentration of more modest red puffin lines coming in further north from Newfoundland and Iceland, black razor-bill lines from Greenland, and shorter green guillemot and auk lines flying in from local fishing grounds all around the British Isles. The whole map would eventually be covered with a mass of coloured lines, possibly ten million of them, all homing in on these islands, and particularly on their western side. During the ocean birds' six-month absence, the food sources around their breeding grounds will have recovered, and all will be in readiness for the vast, noisy busy-ness of another seabird summer.

This is homecoming on an epic scale.

━━─〜─━━

Having drawn an initial blank at the Beacon, I headed towards Mizen Head in my little hire car, stopping briefly in Schull,

* Total combined weight of all the birdlife of any given ecosystem. Interestingly, but irrelevantly here, the fat (1.5 kg) and ubiquitous (35 million) pheasant, artificially bred for shooting, alone counts for about a third of the UK avian biomass.

where I got into a long discussion with the man who was making my coffee about a famous English ornithologist, whose name he couldn't quite remember, who had stayed the previous year at his wife's bed and breakfast for a day or two. Or at least he thought he had. But then possibly, it was the year before. For a while, he held my cup of coffee hostage while he racked his brains to remember the name. Eventually, and in spite of my protestations, he called his wife at home to ascertain exactly who it was and, when that didn't bear fruit, handed me the phone and said it was better if I talked to her direct.

'Oh, that one,' she said eventually, as confused as I was, 'he was an entomologist, and I think he was called Brian.'

By the time I got to Mizen Head, the sole occupant in its 200-bay car park, the weather conditions were close to biblical. They talk of horizontal rain, but half the torrent was actually coming uphill from the sea far below, mixed with salt spray and driven by winds of 50 miles per hour and more. Within seconds, my waterproofs had died as a protective layer: they were designed for heavy showers, not scuba diving. The café on the headland was still closed for another two weeks, with last October's menu staring miserably out through the window; out in the garden, a child's swing swung desolately in the overwhelming greyness. At one point, a brown hare hopped slowly through the deluge about two yards from me, acknowledging my presence with an unhurried shake of the water off its fur. As physically I had reached the south-west tip of Ireland, so metaphorically I had for the time being reached the end of my options. I could climb back into the car and go some place else, or I could stick with the plan and sit it out, waiting for the visibility to lift. I thought momentarily of friends in their warm offices back in England, and deluded myself that they would be as miserable and dissatisfied there as I was sodden and freezing here.

'After all,' I lied aloud to myself either side of a huge sneeze, 'this is a real adventure, isn't it?' The hare had had enough, and lolloped on.

If someone had deliberately set out to make as little shelter available as possible, they could not have made a better job of it than the Mizen Head Café. In the end, only the meagre protection provided by the lee of the café's doorway was available, and I hunched there in my soaking waterproofs and focused the binoculars as best I could through the rain, wind and low cloud, out to sea. I had watched shearwaters enough to know that they were middle- and far-distance birds when seen from the coast, well camouflaged and their presence only really given away by the changing colours they presented during their dynamic soaring. Gulls, fulmars, kittiwakes and gannets flew all around me in abundance, each in their appointed airspace and each in search of their own appointed meal. But no shearwaters.

Sometimes the cloud was so low that it was impossible to distinguish the margins of sea, land and sky, and the shrieking wind comprehensively obscured any possible bird noise. From time to time the mist cleared and I could see far enough out to sea to notice other birds there but, to be honest, they could have been green parakeets or ostriches for all the accurate identification I could muster. Crouched down on arthritic knees while the building that protected me shuddered in the force of the waves pounding far below it, I thought of the string of warm coffee bars further east, stretching back to civilisation. At the same time, the old mantra of my grandmother kept circulating around my brain to the effect that leaving here now 'wouldn't butter any parsnips'. If it annoyed me back then, which it did, it annoyed me even more now. This wasn't about buttering parsnips, it was about finding a wretched bird.

I stuck it out for two hours, maybe three, stuck it out until I could sense the water in my right boot lapping over the tops of my toes. Once in a while, when the cloud cleared, I fancied that I saw shearwaters, equally aware that these were games my mind was playing on me.

There are limits to everything, and right now I needed a hot drink, quite possibly one laced with whiskey.

A few hours later, T72M's final approach to Skomer is like a giant, three-dimensional game of Pelmanism, played out in the dark.

He last saw the island late the previous August on a calm, moonlit night as his chick grew fat three feet down her burrow, but he is returning seven months later in a strong, wet south-westerly wind, which is exactly how he wants it. In the interval, he may have travelled the equivalent of twice around his planet, of which only a third will have been migratory, the balance made up of daily feeding trips. He may have done this full circuit 20 or 30 times already in his lifetime (the evidence suggests that shearwaters only stop breeding when they finally die), so the landmarks will be familiar to him, nudging him into small directional changes as he passes each one. The extraordinary thing is not so much that he found his way out to his million-square-mile wintering grounds last autumn, but that he will accurately navigate his way back in the pitch dark to a burrow entrance no larger than a side plate in time for the breeding season.

Examine the beak of T72M and, for that matter, the beak of any of the 125 species of albatrosses, petrels, storm petrels and shearwaters, and you will quickly notice prominent nostril-like tubes set on the top of the bill where it joins his skull. You might even think them a little odd on a seabird, but they are an important part of our story. These tubes are for the chemoreception that leads to his sense of smell and, through that, to distant food sources and possibly to his burrow itself. (The base of the tube is also used for excreting salt from the seawater that forms his exclusive liquid diet.) He rarely, if ever, rises more than fifteen metres above the waves, even when soaring, so he can't rely, as the stork or eagle can, on a slowly shifting earth map below. At his average height and speed, T72M is watching the sea pass by two metres below him at the rate of fourteen metres per second, hour after hour, day after day, a blurred mass of grey, green and white.

Having been absent from our story for the best part of six months, Ronald Lockley's observations of his first full spring on Skokholm in 1929 become once again a keystone of the architecture of our modern understanding of the Manx shearwater. From the first days of February, when the early returning outliers were driven back out to sea by an intense, month-long cold snap, Lockley was out with his arriving birds each night, and often out among their coastal rafts in his boat in the early evenings. He saw how T72's forebears were silent, almost tame, on the water, and watched the short-winged, footless darting motions of their underwater swimming; he noted the difficulty they had on windless days, and how they would have to take off like a swan, running across the surface to create a wind of their own. He noted how the quietness of the colony on those February evenings was replaced by the 'bedlam nights' of March, and how they avoided coming to land, if they could, until the moon had gone, and wind and rain were in the air. He recorded the clumsy accuracy with which they would land close to a specific burrow, *their* burrow, and proceed towards it without delay or reconnaissance. Many wives would have wished him luck with all this, left him to it and thought him mad, but Doris was made of sterner stuff and, as often as not, was out there with him.

By closely following the six pairs in the immediate vicinity of his farmhouse, Lockley was an admiring voyeur of the courting, pairing and – if he possibly could – copulating of the shearwater couples. He developed the technique, still used today, of digging vertical inspection hatches into the business end of the long burrows, so that he could observe all this, and everything that followed, with minimal disruption; and he came up with little obstacles, such as twin matchsticks stuck in the ground at the entrance, that the birds would unwittingly knock down while exiting the burrow, telling him if they were in or out. And while he made small concessions towards their immediate welfare, such as using red-filtered torches to avoid dazzling them, he generally continued with the robust methods that natural history research embraced at the time. His reaction, for example, to accidentally killing a shearwater while firing his gun at a more distant rabbit was simply to send the unfortunate bird's corpse off to his friend H.F. Witherby to scrutinise under a microscope and determine its sexual maturity at the time of its martyrdom.*

T72M, like his male counterparts in other pairings, will tend to arrive back at the colony a few days ahead of his mate, and because his arrival in the vicinity of Skomer will likely be in the daytime, he will kill the hours until moonless dark by rafting up with others off the coast, and biding his time. Having bred successfully the previous season, he will not be among the earliest arrivers back at Skomer, a privilege generally reserved by birds that failed to raise a chick the year before. He knows that he will have to reclaim last year's burrow, to which he will be instinctively drawn, and may even have to fight for it, before he begins the task of making good any damage that may have been done over the stormy winter months. Contrary to appearances, shearwaters are good burrowers on their own account, and by April the underside of parts of the island starts to look like the battlefield at Vimy Ridge, with shafts being dug hither and thither, and oftentimes straight into a neighbouring burrow, with predictable results.

His biggest problem is likely to involve rabbits. Unlike him, the rabbit has not been drawn down to the South Atlantic over

----

* H.F. Witherby, founding editor of *British Birds*, prime mover in what became the British Trust for Ornithology (BTO) and, ultimately, one of the quiet intelligence heroes of the 1940 Dunkirk evacuation.

the winter; far from it, it has spent some of the intervening time looking for better accommodation which, as often as not, will comprise a well-maintained shearwater burrow, so T72M's first task may well be evicting a creature twice his size, four times his weight, and the possessor of long ears and a fluffy tail. Once he has seen to that, and before he can get on with the basic business of DIY, he may have to fight off puffins, who are often drawn to the same burrow, and then other shearwaters, some of which may be previous generations of his own children.* All of this he tackles with some enthusiasm and enormous noise, and all to ensure that the arrival of T72F is as cordial as possible. With a little over five months needed between copulation and fledging, and with early-season breeding rewarded with markedly higher success rates than later on, he is rightly keen to get on with it.

For a time, T72M is a one-man work party, chiselling away at the burrow wall with his beak, scrabbling the debris out behind him with his webbed feet† and dragging in scraps of vegetation to make the whole thing more comfortable.[4] By and large, shearwater marriages last from one season to the next (unless death or divorce intervene – the latter, it seems, in about 12% of cases), and the process of getting back together again is

----

* It is surprisingly common to find a substantial burrow that hosts a shearwater down the left-hand tunnel, a puffin down the right-hand one, an uneasy looking rabbit somewhere in the middle, and an interested black-backed gull parked on a rock just outside.

† Lockley loved the fact that his own hens, normally shy of straying too far from home, used to wander far and wide at this time of year to take advantage of the dust baths provided by the shearwater's housekeeping.

a balancing act between leaving it as long as possible to depart the feeding grounds, yet not too late to get hold of the best real estate. Old marriage or new courtship, it makes no difference: he needs to make the very best use of the coming nights.

⌐

At the Organico Café in Bantry, where I had gone to dry myself off and take stock, I was once again asked what had brought me to the area.

'Ah. You'll be needing to speak to John from the kitchen,' said the owner, once I had told her. 'He knows his birds.' John duly surfaced with a dishcloth over his shoulder, and John, indeed, knew his birds. Rather more than Dermot, if I am to be honest.

'Dursey Island,' he said, pointing on the map at a speck of land comically far down one of the longest peninsulas in Ireland. 'They were seeing them off there over the weekend.'

This was hot information, but I pointed out to him its twin weaknesses of being 50 miles away, and an inaccessible island in a storm.

'You'll be fine,' he said assertively, and to my surprise. 'The road's good, and there's a cable car.' As much as Dermot had been vague and imaginative, John was precise and his advice was based, it seemed, on real-time information.

'Fine' is a relative term, and more than an hour and a half of winding roads later, and yet another deserted car park, I saw his point. Ireland's only cable car, more of a wooden box hanging precariously between two pylons, had been built in 1968 to get the handful of residents and their livestock reliably out and back over the ferocious 300-metre-wide Dursey Sound. It was done to help sustain the island community, even if the fact that the population had fallen from 56, when it was built, to two today, suggests that access just might not be the only issue for potential residents.

I was the day's sole passenger and, with the exception of a friendly white-bibbed black cat who accompanied me for a section of my six-mile walk, I largely had the place to myself. Dursey Island, which announces itself with enthusiastic marketing acumen as the last place in Europe on which the sun sets, gave me an extraordinary sense of freedom and wildness. From the scarecrow in his wet oilskins pointing the way to the end of the island, to the acrobatic choughs and fulmars, I relished the intense solitude that once might have unnerved me. The rain was less all-pervading than it had been at Mizen Head, meaning that my body was merely soaked, and with a core temperature only marginally down on its optimum. The key thing was that the visibility had improved, and I eventually found myself a vantage point high above the sea, and started my watch. Alone on an island, staring down at seas that would be more in place 9,000 miles to the south.

Flap. Flap. Flap. Glide.

Almost immediately I saw them, four or five of them, Manx shearwaters, shearing their way eastwards a couple of hundred yards out to sea with that familiar lightness that had been so much a part of my previous summer. The facility with which these birds were flying over the wild ocean was in stark contrast to the efforts it had taken me to find my way here. They were truly, in that most misused of expressions, in their element. This was not a journey of lonely hardship or an unwelcome immersion in wilderness, as it would be for another creature; it was the current perfect end-point of 120 million years of evolution.

Each of these birds had put tens of thousands of miles behind them since they had last been in these parts, maybe a full 1,500 hours on the wing, the equivalent of two complete months airborne. During that time, the temperature around them would have ranged by around 40 degrees between, say, the sunny seas off Uruguay and the freezing fog banks of Newfoundland. They would have experienced anything from the flat and oily calms off equatorial Africa to hurricane-force winds a few thousand miles north on their way home. And they would have handled with phlegmatic understanding the subtle changes of diet that each unfolding piece of ocean presented them, because that is what the best travellers do. Every morning, another sea; every night, another horizon.

Since their departure last autumn, they would never have been as far as you might think from the evidence of human beings. Maybe they have seen the crowded beaches and pleasure boats of southern Europe, the hills of Morocco, the oil rigs off Angola; they may have spotted the rusty red trawlers bucking around in mid-Atlantic, the low plains of Patagonia, the noisy whale-watching craft off Valdés, the flaring gas outlets off Venezuela and the cruise ships in the Caribbean winter; perhaps they spied out to their left one night the neon-lit demarcation of the Floridian shore, the little coasters butting their way into Chesapeake Bay and, later on, the fog-bound industrial fisheries on the icy Newfoundland Grand Banks. By the time they eventually swung to the right out across the wide Atlantic Ocean, they only had about 5% of their migratory round trip left.

Flap. Flap. Flap. Glide. The uniformity of direction suggested that these were, indeed, wanderers reaching the final stages of an epic journey rather than recent arrivals out for a feed, and it thrilled me. The concept of 'coming home' is an immensely powerful one for all creatures, as embedded in our souls as it is in the literature of our lives, and I just sat in the wet and the gathering gloom as more and more of them passed. Never a crowd, but never an empty sky, these were, collectively, the most physical antidote to a world that humans have tried to make virtual. Here, on the tantalising edgelands between their world and ours, the shearwaters were flying from the relative safety of the sea into the daily danger of the land, and what I was seeing was the last hurrah of their carefree good times.

Mindful that the operator had a home to go to, and that I had a long drive to somewhere or other, I walked quickly back across the island towards the scarecrow, cat and cable car.

The land close to T72M's burrow would have been the last bit of ground he touched, with a gap of around 196 days between his last visit and this one. After 50,000 miles of precision navigation, he will touch down, maybe this evening, more or less precisely where he last took off from dry land.

They were back. Whatever else the elements threw at me, the shearwaters were back.

10. THE LEGEND
AND THE EGG

April/May, Skomer Island

Parenthood remains the greatest single preserve of the amateur.
ALVIN TOFFLER

It took many attempts to kill off Rasputin.

My grandmother's menagerie of birds was based on a slightly arbitrary version of 'approved' versus 'disapproved'. 'Approved' was in the form of Mr and Mrs Dick, the chaffinches who ate off the breakfast table each morning, and Laurel and Hardy, the gulls up on the roof. 'Disapproved' came in the shape of Rasputin, the resident hooded crow, who terrorised all comers by swooping down on them from the Scots pine by the house, until I removed him from the gene pool one morning while no one was at home, with the old .410 shotgun that lived upright in the larder underneath the shelves of Lyle's black treacle and Tennent's lager.

I knew that I shouldn't do it, even as I removed the old gun from its canvas sleeve, but the breaking of the gun, the insertion of the cartridge, the drawing back of the safety catch, the mounting of the gun into my teenage shoulder, and the swinging through of the barrels against the grey sky until they passed and overtook Rasputin, were driven by a primal urge, I suppose, to show myself that I, too, could potentially fill a cooking pot. The last faint vestiges of my innate hunter-gatherer were making themselves felt while they could, competing for my confused teenage soul with Bob Dylan, the Socialist Workers Party and various acne treatments. The low-velocity echo boomed back at me from the rocks over the other side of Loch Caol, and Rasputin fell spiralling, almost as if in slow motion, into the bracken below.

For a second or two, I didn't fully comprehend the sweet scariness of my success, or know what I was going to do. To me, one hooded crow was very much like another, but an unauthorised use of the 'house' gun was a potentially very volatile development. At the very least, the evidence had to be got rid of. On the other side of the cottage, where the little field dropped away sharply down to the loch, there was a low granite cliff called 'The Great Porridge', where bones and fish heads from the kitchen that couldn't go on the compost or into the dustbin would be thrown into the water below for the tide to do its business. I stood on the peak of the rock and hurled Rasputin's lifeless grey-black corpse out into the low-tide mud,

where it lay accusingly among the emerald seaweed in a cruciform shape, waiting for the sea to once again occupy the little
bay and take it away.

As much as I knew that she need never know, I knew even
more that I couldn't tell my grandmother a direct lie, as to do
so was simply to say that all those years of trust had counted
for nothing. Facing the music was a rite of passage with her,
and her relative frailty in no way masked a towering temper
that I now prepared myself to face.

'Was he flying when you shot him?' was her simple response
when I owned up to the killing after her return. 'So long as he
was, and it was a sporting shot, I will forgive you.' Even to us
children who were used to her robust ways, the period of grief
was a remarkably short one. Perhaps she was mindful of what
the 'hoodies' did to weakened lambs in the spring, and was
happy to see them controlled.

Anyway, it was high summer, which meant that the next
Rasputin duly sidled into the vacated territory a day or so later,
which tended to be the way with her birds. It turned out that
it was only the names that were constant, the birds themselves
merely adopting and then leaving them over our childhood
years. The birds, just like the names of the different sphagnum
mosses on the moor behind the Ardfenaig sheep fank and the
seals in Knockvologan Bay, were part of a process of sustained
education in the natural world, and we were encouraged to
learn as much as we could about them. After all, studying a
chaffinch that is sitting eighteen inches in front of you on the
rim of an earthenware sugar bowl is more rewarding by far
than reading about it in the Ladybird book of garden birds.

Even more so when it is eating stale peanuts from your hand in a state of apparent carelessness.

But the one thing that we were never allowed to do was to anthropomorphise them, to attribute human traits to the creatures whose appearances punctuated our lives in those Hebridean summers. They were wild animals, lower than us, and we had a duty to respect and look after them, but not to pretend they were in any way like us.

'Those fulmars,' she had explained to me back on the high cliffs above Carsaig Bay earlier that summer, 'they just come to the cliff, lay their egg, look after it and then forget the chick for ever. I sometimes think it would be rather easy if we did the same thing.' Even at that young age, I could spot that five decades of hurt was wrapped up in that enigmatic comment. Preoccupied with helping her husband win the war, it was more or less the approach that she had taken to motherhood with her own daughters, when they were little girls in the early 1940s. As children, we subconsciously understood that the inspirational grandmother was, as much as anything, simply making up for being a lousy mother.

'What about love?' I asked, as I was only a little way along the road to cynical adulthood at the time. 'Don't they love the thing that the egg is going to become? Like us and babies?'

'Love's got nothing to do with it,' she replied. 'It's their duty.'

I'd never thought of eggs as duty before, but teenagers can get used to most things, given time.

Not much in current British natural history is listed as 'of no immediate concern', but, for now, the Manx shearwater and its single annual egg is a happy exception.

More as a precaution, and as a statement of how incredibly difficult it is to conduct a census on a bird that divides its time between being far out to sea and deep down in a hole, the Manx shearwater is on the 'amber list' of Birds of Conservation Concern, unlike puffins, arctic skuas and kittiwakes, for example, which are on the red list. One of the criteria for the amber rating is that it has at least 50% of its breeding population in ten or fewer sites, and another is that the UK is host to over 80% of the world population, statements more about potential fragility than an existing problem. The main breeding areas, on Skomer, Skokholm and Rum, are all subject to ongoing scientific investigation, and regular censuses are carried out.[1] Then, by a process of multiplying up, a figure is reached. Depending on whether you are DEFRA* (who think there are currently about 300,000 pairs worldwide) or the scientists (who think that there are around 700,000 pairs in the UK and 100,000 elsewhere), you start to get the picture of a bird that is slowly working its way back into a healthy situation. It is especially exciting to see the change on islands such as Lundy and Canna, which have eradicated all their rats, though less so if you happen to love rats, or are one.

Breeding success for seabirds generally requires three conditions to be met: a reliable food source that lasts out the breeding season, a stable and cooperative marriage, and relative freedom from predators. The Manx shearwater continues to

....

* The UK Department for Environment, Food & Rural Affairs.

be lucky in that it is less choosy about its diet than some other pelagic birds such as the puffin, as we saw earlier, and in that 80% of them breed in three locations that are either rat-free or too high for all but the most adventurous rat to bother with. So, not without a considerable amount of human help, their story remains a good news one.

But they are now entering the critical time of year when just about everything needs to go right for them. Every species of bird has developed its own 'egg strategy', from the sandpipers and stints up in the short Arctic summer that raise two broods simultaneously (one under the female, one under the male) to the Australian brush turkey that just abandons them, once laid, in a heap of rotting vegetation. There is always a reason. Pelagic birds lay but a single egg in a year, as evolution has suggested that the focus on just one chick, rather than multiples, increases the success rate. If that egg fails, not only does the pair not raise a chick that year, but there is a heightened chance that they will 'divorce' as a result, and consequently spend the first part of the following season trying to find another mate. Despite their potential lifespan of 50 years or more, the reality is that the average shearwater dies at between twelve and eighteen years old; and, within that window of just one decade of being a breeder, they might end up raising just five or six broods.

Everything now depends on the next twenty weeks.

~

At my boarding school, there was a clever time not to arrive back on the premises from an illicit evening out, and that was anywhere between 9.00pm, when the housemaster started on his rounds, and 11.00pm, when he went to bed. The signal for approaching safety was the light going out in his bedroom window, which indicated that he had finally stopped reading Lipsey's *Economic Principles* and was turning his thoughts to well-earned rest. Thus the optimum time to break back in was about 11.30pm, when he would be fast asleep and starting to dream perhaps of winning a house cup, or what lay behind the long decline of the British motor industry.

T72M is faced with much the same set of factors when he finally arrives back on Skomer. If he arrives back on land too early, he will attract the unwelcome, and possibly fatal, interest of black-backed gulls and sundry birds of prey; and if he arrives too late, he won't have time to do his night's work before he has to head back out to sea four hours later. The ideal night for T72M is a dark, moonless and rainy one, with a light wind, the ideal time is a couple of hours after last light, and the ideal place for him to wait for it is out on the bit of sea immediately below his part of the colony. After his 9,000-mile voyage, he will land quietly on the sea among the other rafting shearwaters from his part of the colony, and await night-time. To observe these sometimes vast congregations is to see the nomad at his most peaceful and his quietest.

After such a monumental journey, it is an understated arrival.

Shearwater breeding behaviour is a bit like a self-adjusting nut, where the earlier they start, the more likely they are to raise a chick to fledging, and the less they succeeded the previous year, the earlier they start in the next one. Three-quarters of shearwater marriages continue into the following year, but, as generations of humans have discovered, a second marriage is not in itself a guarantee of harmony and success. The fundamental equation is that, in order for the chick to fledge before the equinoctial storms of late September, everything needs to be ready by mid-April. Readiness, in this case, means pairing or re-pairing with a mate, claiming or re-claiming the burrow, and then doing the essential DIY jobs that make it an acceptable home. T72F, his previous partner, is only a few days behind him and drawing inexorably closer to the island.

'During this pre-laying period the burrow is prepared for laying,' writes Mike Brooke, who spent most of the summers of his twenties with his nose close to, or down one. 'The shearwater bill chisels at the burrow walls. Next the feet, with a scrabbling action that often leaves two scoured tramlines along the burrow, send loosened soil and other winter debris through the entrance. Finally the shearwaters, now filthy thanks to their spring cleaning endeavours, drag in available scraps of vegetation to form a crude pad to receive the egg.'[2]

Ronald Lockley talked about them 'attacking the soft earth with their pickaxe bills', and observed that some pairs were a good deal more picky than others when it came to an acceptable standard of residence. Indeed, some don't seem to need a burrow at all. One pair set up home year after year on the floor of a long-disused monk's stone cell on Great Skellig, off Ireland, and Lockley himself had them beneath the boards of his farmhouse. Judging from the frequent and bloody fights that take place in the colony at this time of year, there is a clear hierarchy, and therefore value, in what is considered prime real estate and what isn't. Brooke's research further indicated that there was on average a six-week gap between the first arrival of the male and the laying of an egg, and that a large part of this gap was spent out at sea, fishing. At the end of the process, T72F needs to be in good enough condition to lay an egg that is around 15% of her own bodyweight, the equivalent of a 9 kg human baby.

The colony is ramping up a little more every day, and darkness brings Lockley's 'bedlam' noises back once again, a sound that has haunted the human imagination for millennia.

The myths of the shearwater may start all the way back in the *Odyssey*, in which the hero is rescued from a terrifying storm by an *aithyia*, a mysterious seabird that gives him a magic veil to draw him through it. Academics and historians have long argued what bird an *aithyia* might have been, lurching from gull to heron to curlew to just about anything else with a pulse that flies, before settling on the shearwater on the basis that it is first a seabird, and secondly, very noisy at night.* And the shearwater would have been well served had myth and legend stopped at that point, a bird of heroism and sanctuary. As it was, things went steadily downhill from there.

Seabird myths evolved to suit the narratives of the communities they came from. Thus, for example, Hawaiian white

---

* There is a theme here. My favourite Latin bird name of all, *Diomedea exulans* (the wandering albatross), comes from another Greek hero and his troubled travels.

terns only became birds of homecoming because they naturally gravitated towards islands and were therefore logically a bird you were likely to see as you approached land from a long voyage; tropicbirds became messengers of the gods, albatrosses followed ships because they represented the souls of dead sailors, and puffins had power over the winds and weather. The issue for the shearwater is that it has generally bred as far from those human communities as it can, which means that man's first intersection with it has tended to be deep in the night, and as a series of unearthly calls, normally issuing forth from the tops of cliffs high above the often superstitious sailors who happened to be listening to them. Very quickly, the harmless shearwater became a symbol of bad weather at best, and approaching, or actual, death at worst.

Famously, an invading horde of Vikings heard the noise from the hills above them on the coast of Rum, the same hills I had visited with Tim Guilford the previous summer. Pausing briefly to point out that no one could possibly have overheard the mountain-top birds from the coast a minimum of two miles away, even down the prevailing wind, the legend evolved that this was a land of trolls, and best avoided. Back to their homelands went the ships, carrying with them the notion that these were islands of danger, and of unthinkable creatures. To this day, the hill called Trolleval is one of the main breeding sites in the birds' northern stronghold.

A few hundred miles south on the Isle of Man, and a few hundred years later, the same strand of publicity was developing. Here's a description of their voice from 1731: 'The spirits which haunted the coasts have originated in this noise, described as infernal. The disturbed spirit of a person ship-wrecked on a rock adjacent to this coast wanders about it still, and sometimes makes so terrible a yelling that it is heard at an incredible distance. They tell you that houses even shake with it; and that, not only mankind, but all the brute creation within hearing, tremble at the sound. But what serves very much to increase the shock is that, whenever it makes this extraordinary noise, it is a sure prediction of an approaching storm. At other times the spirit cries out only, "Hoa, hoa, hoa!" with a voice little, if anything, louder than a human one.'[3]

The bird's PR problem didn't stop in northern Europe, nor with the Manx shearwater. Wherever shearwaters were found, which is off just about every ice-free ocean coast in the world, their night-time bedlam cries created the prism through which people would think about them. To the Maoris, they were birds of mourning, and sometimes the Devil Bird; to Muslim sailors, they were simply the bird of death, and to their French counterparts they were '*âmes damnées*', the souls of the damned. The ultra-secular Richard Dawkins delighted in telling the story of a fellow undergraduate who, while camping on Rum, thought he had heard the devil calling – which had, in turn, led him to eventual ordination.[4]

In a species' relationship with the human race, it helps if you look cute, or at least do cute things. In fact, at some stage, someone will inevitably do a PhD proving conclusively that cute-looking animals (say the koala bear) cheat extinction for longer than the less cute ones (say the harmless but unprepossessing and now extinct Tasmanian tiger). The shearwater isn't particularly cute: it just dovetails neatly and unfussily into the natural world around it, and flies for ever. Of all the 11,200 or so bird species out there, the shearwater perhaps comes closest to complete affinity with the elements around it. If the puffin looked like a blackbird, it would be just another bird flying off its cliff-top home to go and collect some sand eels. And if the shearwater had the face of a clown and did its stuff in the daytime, it would be on every seabird conservation poster ever produced.

Eventually, all legends tend to get mixed up with religion and food, and so it is for the Manxie. On the Isle of Man, as elsewhere, the convenient fact of their being marine feeders, and therefore having a fishy tang to their flesh, enabled the Catholic Church to authorise them to be eaten during the Lent fast, much like the unfortunate capybara is occasional Friday fare in Latin America. At all times of the breeding season, and in all areas of their range, shearwaters became a staple, tradeable part of our diet. Whether it was on Man, the Faroes or Iceland, all places where a good living was to be made, or in the Scilly Isles, where feudal rents were paid in dead shearwaters back in the thirteenth century, the birds were often little more than a commodity. After all, this was a world where rent could be paid on St Kilda by bags of fulmar feathers, and sailors habitually made tobacco pipes out of the tibia of albatrosses. As late as the 1960s, great shearwaters were a convenient packed meal for the egg gatherers of Tristan da Cunha, plucked from their burrows, boiled, and supplemented by rockhopper penguins' eggs.[5]

In 2019, the seabird ecologist for the Scilly Wildlife Trust told me that she had received a mysterious email from someone in Germany, asking for a piece of shearwater eggshell, or a feather, to be sent over. When asked what she wanted it for, she received the reply that the correspondent was a homeopathist, and that she used minute quantities of it in potions to treat people going on long journeys. Innocent enough, we agreed, but you cannot help but wonder where the idea came from, and how many birds made their way across the country to satisfy it.

Manx shearwaters are still eaten in various places to this day, but it is highly unlikely that this makes any significant dent in their population. As we shall see in the next chapter, it would take something 400 times smaller than man to manage that.

———

On April 18th, T72M and T72F finally copulate (a word that Lockley seemed to delight in when discussing his shearwaters), and on May 7th, T72F lays a large egg deep in her burrow, probably on a bed of grassy detritus that they have both brought in.

Geoff didn't know about any of this, out here on the empty, daytime shearwater lawns.

Geoff had come to Skomer for the day, he told me, because he felt he had a decent chance to add a few rare vagrants to his list; something, for example, like a Sabine's gull, a grey phalarope or a melodious warbler.

'You never quite know what's going to make its way onto your list here,' he said genially, as I stopped to pass the time of day on a walk round the island. 'I picked up a common rosefinch in 2015, and a long-tailed skua later the same year.' He was in combat fatigues and was nursing the eyepiece of an enormous Swarovski ATS telescope as if he somehow wanted me to notice it and talk about it with him. He gestured towards an empty rock to his right, silently inviting me to share the moment with him.

'I left Andover just after three this morning, you know,' he went on, as if it somehow explained everything. 'I always stop for a coffee at the services on the A48 at Carmarthen. I was in Norfolk at the weekend to see if I could get me a pectoral sandpiper.'

'And could you?' I asked.

'Sadly not,' he said, and scanned the cliff edge with a tiny pair of binoculars while he spoke. 'But I got a western osprey in Rutland Water for my troubles the weekend before, which kind of made up for it.' I briefly wondered whether there was a Mrs Geoff and, if so, what she made of it all.

'And why are *you* here?' he asked after a while, trying not to make it sound like an accusation to some unprincipled competitor. The implication was that no one would conceivably come to this island and do this sort of stuff if they weren't also furtively adding to their own list.

'Shearwaters,' I replied neutrally.

'What? Balearics or something?'

'No. Just good old plain Manxies.' I explained that I was following them for a year, and writing about them; that I was here to live among the bedlam calls at night, and the evening rafts. I looked into his eyes and saw only the confusion of a child being shown a new conjuring trick.

'I don't know about all that detail stuff,' he said sympathetically, after a pause. 'I generally like to get somewhere, see the bird, tick it off and then get the hell out. No point in hanging

around using up valuable time. Once you've positively identified it, I'm afraid a bird's just a thing with two wings and a
beak to me.'

We sat together quietly and looked out at the vastness of
the shining sea, at one with each other as much as we were
divided within our common cause. If he represented the mili-
tant activist wing of ornithology, and I its sleepy cultural
backwaters, we still had a shared passion for those 'two wings
and a beak' of his. After a while, Geoff unscrewed the top off
a large camouflaged flask, and wordlessly handed me a beaker
of sweet tea. Wordlessly, too, I handed him my open packet of
Cheesy Wotsits. In the birding world, we never underestimate
the bonding power of a brew, just as we never leave home
without a woolly hat. The Cheesy Wotsits are optional, like a
fine brandy after dinner.

Emboldened, I asked him what his cup-final moment had
been in a life of twitching and, for a second or two, childlike
innocence seeped through him.

'A shorelark,' he said. 'In a car park in Great Yarmouth.
Back in 2013. I drove 170 miles to see it, and it got me to
350 British species for the year for the first time. I nearly cried.'
For a second, I tried to imagine him crying, out there in the
cold North Sea wind overlooking the grey mudflats, with great
tears rolling off his stubbly chin onto the disruptive patterns
of his combat jacket.

Then the arrival of something that momentarily might have
been, but eventually wasn't, a red-breasted flycatcher allowed
us both to make our apologies, he to look out for those Sabine's
gulls, and me to get back to my egg.

And it is a large egg; indeed, if your breakfast egg was of the same proportions relative to the size of the bird that laid it, it would be four times as big, and weigh half a kilo. If all goes well, T72, who is plying her student way thousands of miles south and west, will soon have a sibling from the same genetic lineage, albeit one she will in all probability never meet.

Lockley wrote movingly about this time of the year. He would sit out in the dark behind the cottage, listening to the individual calls of his shearwaters returning from a day's foraging and communicating with an underground partner, wondering which one was which. For him, the dark was not so much an obstacle in the way of seeing his birds, as an opportunity to see them differently. And with them, the myriad other birds that were transiting his island high above on their night-time migrations northwards: the whistling of the whimbrel heading to the Shetlands; a 'gaggling' skein of white-fronted geese 'bound for the tundra of the far north', calling to each other all the while. Beyond that, all he could hear was the sound of their wings hissing through the air somewhere high above him in the blackness.

It is hard to exaggerate the lengths that a shearwater goes to in the interests of the unborn chick, from the restlessness it first feels in the South Atlantic in mid-January, right up to the moment that the chick is unceremoniously abandoned at the end of August. We talk as humans of being in or out of our comfort zone, and we need to keep remembering that a shear-water's sweet spot is to be found far out at sea, not on dry land, and that each trip to the colony carries some underlying element of additional risk. They breed on land only because evolution hasn't yet found them a way to do that out at sea. At sea, they are safe.

For the last eighteen days before laying, T72F has been shearing the waters of the Atlantic continental shelf, alert for the upwind signs of DMS gas that will lead her to the food she needs to reach peak condition. Since she spends about four hours a day in flight, with the remainder either foraging or resting on the water, it is likely that she will cover as much as 3,000 or 4,000 miles on her trip.[6] Her mate has been doing the same, but more locally and often returning to the colony between feeds. He will take the first long stint of incubation duty once she has laid her egg, so he needs to be in decent condition too, but he also needs to be ready to defend the burrow from the unwelcome attentions of unsettled pairs, which is possibly why he comes back as often as he does. Research has not yet confirmed whether, as it is with many other bird species, an opportunity for some extra-marital sex isn't one of the other drivers that brings him home with such regularity.*

Nor is it for me to enter the debate as to whether birds have the capacity for love; but, in comparison with the Laysan albatross and its ritual pair dance, for example, or with the scarlet macaw, the shearwater seems to have quite a robust and practical attitude to relationships. If they work, great, but

---

* The waved albatross seems to be the naughty boy in this respect, with up to a quarter of all the chicks in one piece of genetic research not fathered by the relevant husband. (Dr M. Brooke, anecdotal)

if they don't, simply move on. Lockley would have demurred, of course, and referred to 'the amorous billing and cooing when they would caress each other with their bills' each dark night when they met at the burrow, but then he was an incurable old romantic.

The fascinating notion of there being an element of negotiation and coordination to all this preparation is not yet well understood, but it is nonetheless highly likely. Among birds, zebra finches are known to use different vocal communications for different reasons during the incubation period,[7] and it is probable that the same sort of thing happens with shearwaters, during the hour or so of calling when they are together at the burrow. The latest research indicates that it might revolve around how long the foraging bird should head out to sea for, and it seems to be based on the current condition and mass of both the leaving bird and the one left behind. The weaker the foraging bird, the longer the replenishing journey should be, but if the incubating bird is weak as well, the former knows that it must compromise on the length of its trip, so as to give the other an equal chance to recover. This is in stark contrast to most partnerships in nature, where a high degree of marital selfishness exists.

The first pair of shearwaters that Lockley observed back in the 1930s, Adam and Ada, were, in all probability, the first pair that had ever been carefully observed by anyone. Night after night, once the egg had been laid, Lockley would return to the burrow, open the inspection hatch, check which of the two were sitting on the egg and – above all – see if the egg had hatched. He noted that one or other bird would head back out to sea for days at a time, sometimes as many as five, while the other kept its lonely vigil underground, maintaining the egg at the right temperature. From about 28 days in, Lockley began to panic that the egg was addled and would never hatch. Each evening, he counted the days off against what he knew of other breeding birds' incubation times: 30 days for the white stork, 35 days for the osprey, 38 days for the mute swan, 40 days for the golden eagle, and 48 days for the massive vulture. It was not until the 51st day, with Ada on duty, that Lockley picked up the egg and shook it, expecting to hear the rattle that would indicate it was addled, only to find, to his delight, that it was 'pipped'.

'A network of cracks had appeared at the big end,' he wrote. 'I fancied that Ada looked more maternal that morning (I couldn't wait for the evening on these important days). Certainly, she was anxious, and did not move readily from the egg when I slipped my hand into the nest. The chick called faintly from the egg and Ada, usually so silent when visited, gave a little half-strangled cry. And this is not sentiment on my part.' He describes his 'dancing toes as I ran to the house to tell my wife', and how the next morning they finally saw the chick, 'the black, ugly little ball, wet from the shell.'[8]

Thus, after what turned out to be a record length of observed incubation for any British wild bird, arrived Hoofti.

And thus, 80 years later to the day, and a mile or so to the north, arrived T72B.

So far so good.

11. BROWN-COATED KILLERS

August, The West Coast

Down at the bottom of the second glass display cabinet on your left as you walk into the bird department of London's Natural History Museum, you will see a stuffed, yet dignified, great auk. Along with a dodo, a passenger pigeon, a huia and a Caroline parakeet, the auk represents the museum's rather inadequate tribute to the 160 or so species of bird that have gone extinct in the last 200–300 years.

You might stare at it for a while, surprised at the penguin-like size of a bird that you learn was once, recently even, widespread around these Northern Atlantic shores. You might go on to think that a large, flightless and – surely – clumsy bird like this probably had extinction coming to it, and that every large land and sea predator would have been queueing up to hasten its demise. You would be wrong. There was no habitat loss involved, no rising sea temperatures, no shortage of food. There was no imbalance of rival fishing birds, no catastrophic storm, no introduction of aggressive species. All that did for them in the end was mankind's insatiable appetite: appetite for flesh, for fat, for oil, for egg collections and – finally – for feathers in the pretty hats of the fine ladies of London and Paris. By 1850 the last one had gone, killed in Iceland by two people who already knew that it was probably the last one on earth. It turned out that evolution had dealt the great auk a fatal hand in giving it attractive feathers and collectible eggs.

If that stuffed great auk in its glass case in South Kensington tells us anything beyond the sadness of its own story, it hints to us that being a seabird has been a precarious business recently. When the population statistics of observed species is extrapolated to take into account the unobserved ones, it is likely that we have lost around 1 billion birds from the biomass of seabirds since 1960, out of a starting population of 1.5 billion.[1] That's two thirds of all seabirds gone, and all in the evolutionary blinking of an eye. When it comes to causing biomass to decline across the animal life on our shared planet, two thirds

happens to be about par for the course for what our own species can manage, which is quite an achievement when we only
really got going around the time of the industrial revolution.

This matters, because if you extend the population line for
seabirds, you arrive into silence in about 2060.

The Manx shearwater's relative success in the last few
decades is a welcome one, to be sure, but it is also an outlier,
an eddy in the ebb tide of decline. Gulls, kittiwakes, fulmars,
albatrosses and puffins are all going remorselessly in the other
direction. And even T72B, this newest member of a successful
species, as he enters the period of most vulnerability of his life,
has a long and determined list of threats through which he has
to navigate before he flies to the other side of the globe and
gets his first glimpse of the southern oceans.

The shearwater is a robust bird. It can deal with rain, storms,
heat, drought, mist, fog and, of course, darkness. As we have
seen, it is not picky about its food, and can travel far and fast
economically and, if required, resting on the wing. It flies too low
to get involved in wind turbines, swims too deep to get caught
on long-line bait, and generally too shallow to be caught up in
nets. It is used by scientists as a sentinel species, employed to
monitor environmental contamination, as it seems to be able
to absorb reasonable quantities of mercury, selenium, cadmium
and lead without ill effect.[2] But there is nonetheless an ever-
present hierarchy of threat applicable to the breeding shearwater,
and it all starts with man. Without us, there would probably be an
equilibrium, and chapters like this would not need to be written.

The world that greets T72B on his first day alive is dark, earthy, a little bit damp, and probably with an underlying smell of half-processed fish oil. Just the way he will grow to like it, in fact. He is three feet down a burrow, halfway up a steep, east-facing hill, out of the practical range of anyone other than his parents. If he happened to come to the entrance, his view would be of a research hut nearby just down the hill, the sea below and the rigs and cranes of Milford Haven out in the distance. The days are silent, save for the endless crying of the gulls, the wash of the tide on the shingle shore below and, if you listen very carefully, the tiny childish cheeps of a hungry shearwater waiting to be fed. Infant shearwaters are not handsome in any way; after all, even the adoring Lockley termed them 'the black, ugly little ball, wet from the shell'.

This burrow will be his home for the next ten weeks; indeed, it is the only home he will ever have known for the next four or five years. Between now and fledging, his parents will provide all that he needs to develop from the 50-gram unprepossessing ball of fluff that he is now to the half-kilo navigator of the oceans that he will rapidly become. For the first week, one or other parent will be in constant attendance at the burrow, after which he will be on his own during daylight hours which, at this time of year, is three quarters of the time. Their foraging trips are shorter now, and closer to the island, so as to ensure that he is fed regularly. But they do not come back every night, and, if the moon is full and the wind is light, they may well leave him alone for up to three or four days. His diet of half-digested fish is converted efficiently into flesh and mass, and for every three grams he eats, he gains over a gram of weight. Very little is wasted, and therefore the burrow remains surprisingly clean.

The waters and skies around his island of Skomer are the ornithological equivalent of a mega-city, a teeming mass of birdlife on the move. If you aggregate all those coloured lines of inbound migration from earlier in the spring, all the shearwaters, razorbills, guillemots, puffins and storm petrels, and then add to them the resident gulls, gannets, fulmars and kittiwakes, and finally include neighbouring Skokholm Island for good measure, there are almost certainly more than a million birds wheeling and diving their way around the local sky. One way or another, all of them are after fish and yet, at this early point in the season, there is normally plenty to go around to provide the 150 tons that the local cohort of seabirds require on a daily basis.* In terms of food at least, these are the easy days.

And that is precisely why T72B needs to grow and develop so quickly. Because, come September, the seas will be emptier and the living harder, and his parents won't be hanging around to explain why.

———⌐——

When the little ferry sets the new visitor down for their first visit to Skomer Island, their temptation might be to stride out ahead of the crowd so as to be more or less on their own while

....

* Over a breeding season, Skomer and Skokholm seabirds will eat through the equivalent of 5%–6% of the annual seafood consumption of all the humans in the UK.

they walk round the island, the better to observe the wildlife and to recreate the envelope of peace that Ronald Lockley found on neighbouring Skokholm.

Once they are out on the raised moorland that makes up the middle part of the island, they might start to notice something on the paths through the bracken that they have never seen before in all their birdwatching years: corpses. Hundreds of shearwater corpses. Some are just about eviscerated by the workings of the savage beak of a black-backed gull, and some are almost unmarked. What strikes the first-time visitor most powerfully, apart from the regularity of the bodies, is that no other bird is similarly represented: no puffin, no fulmar, no kittiwake. And they might start to think that, for a bird that only comes to land at night when there are no airborne predators around, and with no hunting mammals on this island, this is all rather strange. By the time they have completed the three-mile circuit of the island, they might have seen a hundred or more of these bodies, and they will probably need to be reassured by the warden that this is the expected and acceptable collateral damage of a huge population of breeding pairs of birds on a small island. Which it is. They are simply the ones that came in too early, or went to ground too late; or, wracked with puffinosis,* just lost the strength to get back to their burrow in time. A hundred or so a night out of a third of a million is

....

* A viral infection, much researched but still relatively little understood, similar to myxomatosis in rabbits, which affects a regular 4%–5% of the shearwater population on Skomer and Skokholm, but nowhere else. Presenting as blisters, starting on the webbed feet, it is almost invariably fatal.

a manageable wastage rate in nature, and there is no rational room for sentimentality in the species' largest breeding colony. Indeed, Lockley himself noted 1,500 or so shearwater bodies during the one season that he was moved to count them. Presumably, these included the ones that he accidentally dispatched himself.

Man is only one of a dozen or so creatures on a standard, human-settled North Atlantic island that might harm a seabird, and that is before you start to consider disease, the effects of over-fishing, or long-line fishing, or warming oceans on the movement of fish, or the ingestion of poison through the food chain, or micro-plastics, or flying into the blades of giant offshore wind turbines,* and on it goes. Some threats are quite surprising, like the sheep and red deer that will break and eat seabird eggs for calcium, and even bite the heads off chicks for probably the same reason. Some we would expect, and possibly even find magnificent from our human perspective, like the peregrine or golden eagle (and we probably need to be reminded from time to time that it was only back in the 1820s that a shepherd on Rum was recorded as having shot no fewer than five sea eagles in a day). Some, like the ubiquitous black-backed gull, the raven,† the hooded crow and the skua, we already

....

* Seabird deaths through striking wind turbine blades is a classic example of the genuine conflicts in ecology and conservation. Through trying to reduce the effects of climate change, which benefits all species, an increased number of seabirds will take the hit. Fortuitously, the Manx shearwater generally flies too low to be badly affected, as noted above.
† On Skomer, a number of ravens have learned to enter the dark burrows and drag chicks out.

understand as opportunist predators working the coastal cliffs and breeding grounds of our western isles. Breeding exclusively on islands, the Manxie tends to escape the attentions of weasels, stoats, mink and polecats, unlike mainland-based migrating seabirds, and they don't have to run the gauntlet of French 'sportsmen' or Maltese netters. Some killers are directly related to man's activities, like cats, or people innocently walking their dogs. Even the fish beneath the waves have a go, and many is the bird that has lost part or all of one foot, or both, while innocently rafting up on the surface of the sea.

But one animal alone is a relentless persecutor of the Manx shearwater.

Rattus norvegicus, otherwise variously known as the brown, common, street, sewer, Hanover, Norwegian, Parisian, water, long-tailed or wharf rat, is the shearwater's tormentor-in-chief. Inevitably introduced by nautical man's accidental carelessness, the rat left any number of sinking ships to cause the extinction of seabird colonies on island after island around the world. Homing in on the burrows with the accuracy of a heat-seeking missile, they are genetically programmed to breed and breed until the food source is entirely gone, at which point they move out. A rat reaches sexual maturity in four to five weeks, and typically has six litters of twelve pups a year; follow the mathematical logic, and it begins to dawn on you that a single pair can theoretically become 1,250 rats after a year, and a shade under half a *billion* after three.[3]

The only thing that stops rats taking the whole place over completely is that the one animal they require to spread themselves about in the first place – man – happens also to be the one animal that is relatively effective at controlling them. This is particularly the case on islands, which are simultaneously where most seabirds choose to breed and where it is just about possible to get rid of the rats. Nonetheless, the roll call of islands whose shearwater populations were eradicated reads with the same elegiac sadness as Flanders and Swann's list of Beeching's closed railway stations, and it starts with the island that gave the Manxies their name, Man. Man, the animal not the island, brought the rats to the islands in the first place, and it will be man, as the technological and scientific Pied Piper, who has eventually to lead them out again, if he chooses to. At £500 per hectare of 'control', clearing the Isle of Man of rats would cost a cool £28 million, which suggests that it just might not be a priority in these straitened times.*

In passing, it would be wrong to ascribe all the rodent blame just to rats. While, in one corner of the world, 150 Canna mice (a sub-species that environmentalists were keen to protect when they were ridding Canna of rats) were housed in a zoological

....

* There are exceptions to the unsaid rule that only small islands qualify for eradication schemes. In April 2018, the distinctly large sub-Antarctic island of South Georgia was declared rat-free for the first time for 250 years. It had taken 300 metric tons of poison, £10 million and nearly a decade to achieve it. Even checking it was rat-free had taken six months. Thirty years previously, I had watched a giant rat and a giant skua fight to the finish over some scraps, out in front of our hut. My soldiers placed bets, and the skua won.

Airbnb at Edinburgh Zoo and then re-homed once the job was done, in another (Gough Island in the South Atlantic), a strain of super-mouse has evolved to three times its normal size, and has moved from a vegetarian to a carnivorous diet, the target being the Tristan albatross. Videos of how they do what they do are not for the faint-hearted,* but that particular albatross is heading for extinction if nothing can be done. Once again, the predator came in thanks to man.

The equation is simple enough: if your island has rats, you almost certainly won't have shearwaters; if it doesn't, you might.

On Rum, where the shearwaters' burrows are high up in the mountains of Hallival and Askival, a recent survey[4] arrived at the startlingly precise conclusion that there were 11,844 Norwegian rats on the island, but that the majority of them were based at or near sea level, and that they didn't pose much of a threat to the higher-altitude birds. This is a rare case indeed of the presence of rats not leading directly to the absence of shearwaters.

Not everything that threatens a seabird is as obvious, or as lively, as a rat. A recent survey[5] of the flesh-footed shearwaters that breed on Lord Howe Island off Australia found that the *average* unfledged chick had already ingested between 30 and 40 pieces of plastic waste – from pieces of Lego to biro caps

---

* Available for view on YouTube, if you must. Viewer discretion is advised.

to bottle tops, toy car wheels and balloon clips – before it even had the chance to fly for the first time; the most they found in one bird was 266 pieces (or 64 grams), the equivalent of an average-weight human carrying around an extra ten kilos of trash in their body. Feeding parents seemed to be attracted to the plastic in the water for some reason, almost certainly seeing it as a food source, so it could not even be put down to an occasional mistake, or something that they would eventually learn to avoid.

The time which T72B spent in the egg, and now spends in his burrow, are absolutely critical to his long-term survival, and living on a rat-free, mammal-free, largely human-free island is the best start he could possibly have.

Ironically, though, if you look at all this from the perspective of the neighbouring puffin, 5% of their breeding losses, where colonies are shared with Manx shearwaters, are caused by the shearwater itself, a little-known fact that goes a tiny way to explaining one factor in the relative successes of the two breeds.[6] Manxies might be no match for a 1.8-kilo black-backed gull, but they can quite easily break the egg of an annoying residential rival.

⁓

Back in his burrow on that Skomer hillside, T72B is growing swiftly and strongly to the rhythm of the sea's bounty.

Although he will vibrate his tiny wings to keep himself warm, his instinct is to avoid the lure of the daylight that gleams around the corner of the burrow; daylight, he knows, means danger. Unless a researcher intervenes to weigh or ring him, his first sight of daylight will probably be in ten weeks' time from the sea, or the sky just above it. Given that 90% of the rest of his life will be spent on the sea or in the sky, it is all a fine example of the species' slow and deliberate less-is-more breeding strategy.

On his own, the burrow will be a largely silent place punctuated only by his high-pitched cheeps of hunger. For a select few, it will also feature the silent digital spinning of a cunningly sited webcam.

I'm not quite sure what I was expecting an unfledged shearwater to do in his burrow after the initial bout of intense parental attention had finished, but the answer is, as far as the daylight hours are concerned, almost nothing. Long before dawn, when his parents had made their gull-defying flights back out to sea, he slept with his head held high on his bed of dried grass. Then, for much of the day, he either dozed or stared enigmatically out towards the entrance of the burrow. Sometimes he faced outwards, the view partially obscured by the broken eggshell from which he had recently emerged, and sometimes into the end wall. As evening approached, he might indulge in some low-level preening, and articulate his hunger through a series of tiny cheeps and clicks. It was never until night fell that the real action would start. The first noise would normally come from the entrance of a neighbouring burrow, rather than his, but it was always enough to get him into a state of excitement. Some moonlit evenings, and there were many that spring, neither parent came back at all, and the patient vigil just rolled over into another long day. Lockley used to be amazed just how long a chick could keep going without sustenance after the first week or so of its life, and four or five days was par for the course. You could sense the disappointment, though, or at least thought you could; and, if you listened carefully, you could hear the faint scream of a herring gull above the empty harbour, as the last of the daylight drained out of the western sky.

When relief eventually came, when the rain was in the air and the scudding cloud obscuring the moon, mostly it was one parent, but occasionally both would crowd into the tight burrow. The microphone, set so as to pick up the quietest sounds from the chick and from the world outside, boomed chaotically with the noise of bird greeting bird, bird greeting chick, bird scrambling over bird, and chick demanding to be fed. My locked-down family became used to these sudden intrusions, as I would leave whatever I was doing and sit down to watch the urgent cross-billed lunges of the ravenous chick as its parent regurgitated the half-digested produce of a 300-mile trip, in full payment for the three-day absence. These moments of feeding, intimacy and affection are the single axle around which the shearwater's young life rotates, and they are as close as he will ever be to any bird until, maybe in four or five years, he becomes a parent himself.

Over that month, he became my constant grey companion down in the bottom left-hand corner of my computer screen, while I worked and wrote. Day by day, I felt myself to be a tiny part of the natural drama, the last scene of which would be for him to propel himself from a nearby rock into the September night a few weeks from now. Each dawn, I would clasp a mug of tea in both hands and watch him doing more or less nothing until I had drained the last drop; as I drank my morning coffee, I would stop what I was doing and just observe him. Same at lunch time, and same at tea.

Inadvertently, the bird probably became a bigger part of my life as a virtual presence in my study than if I had spent June on his island, weighing him once a week.

~~~

Happily, man's particular genius has been to invent ways of solving the problems that he himself has created, and the story of the last hundred years of conservation has almost as much in it to celebrate, at least in terms of human endeavour, as to condemn.

Active conservation has many parents, but a good start point is Octavia Hill's London sitting room one evening in 1878, when the first recognisable stirrings of the National Trust emerged and, with it, the notion that nature and heritage needed the protection of more than just luck. Eleven years later, and 200 miles north, what was to become the Royal Society for the Protection of Birds (RSPB) took its first breath, followed by the Nature Reserve movement (1926), the National Parks (1949),[7] the island restoration projects (1962), the fishing quota system (1984), and marine conservation zones (2013). All of these have in one way or another, and together, helped out British seabirds, moderating their declines, but perhaps none more so than the invasive species exterminations that have come under the aegis of the island restoration projects.*

....

* It is less hazardous, in PR terms, getting rid of unloved rats to protect seabird colonies than it proved to be 'removing' the alien hedgehogs that were decimating the wader population on the islands of Uist in the Outer Hebrides. So much so that Scottish Natural Heritage spent £2,679,362 rehoming 2,441 hedgehogs to keep Brian May and

Getting rid of invasive species that man himself has introduced, generally deliberately, has had to become an expensive branch of conservation these days, since the newcomers mostly have a devastating effect on the existing residents. This is normally because the new arrival has the unfair advantage of having no natural predators or pests, and is able to grow without constraint in its new environment. Whether in the form of a plant, like the ubiquitous Japanese knotweed, an insect like the Asian hornet, or a fish like the topmouth gudgeon, not to mention all the cats, rabbits, grey squirrels, mink and others, they impose themselves brutally on the locals and change the balance of everything. Indeed, Britain's ten million cats, many of them paradoxically owned by conservationists and bird-lovers, account for 27 million songbirds each year.[8] And that is a particularly conservative estimate.

In the early 1950s, mankind wearily accepted that something needed to be done, and the first island eradication schemes were introduced, starting in New Zealand. It all grew from there and, in the name of rebalancing, invaders as diverse as goats, hedgehogs, rabbits, possums and feral cats have been removed from over 500 islands worldwide, not to mention the rats. Accidents can and do happen, of course, such as the infamous killing of 46 protected bald eagles on the Aleutian Islands in 2009, and not every extermination is universally welcomed.

A major study in 2000 on the Shiants, a small Scottish island group between Lewis and the mainland, showed that

....

Joanna Lumley off their backs, at a rate of £1,097 per hedgehog. (*Daily Mirror*, 2017)

the seaside population of black rats (*Rattus rattus*) that had been delivered there courtesy of a shipwreck a hundred years before, fed, thrived, bred and over-wintered rather better than their inland cousins,[9] and were wreaking havoc with the Manx shearwaters. In a classic example of the dichotomies faced by conservationists, for a while the black rats, of which this was one of only two naturalised populations in the whole of Britain, were protected. Then, in 2015/16, after the Shiants ticked all the scientific criteria boxes in an earlier study,[10] the sentiment changed and extermination was planned. The Shiants are a very sensitive and special group of islands, and the owner a highly enlightened steward for them, so great care was taken by all parties to ensure that the essential untouched nature of their wildness was kept intact, meaning no signboards and no long-term trace of the operation. Within six months, storm petrels were seen once again on the cliffs, and after two years, Manx shearwaters were again heard at night over the islands. The same has happened on Canna, Ramsey, Lundy, and St Agnes and Gugh in the Scilly Isles with the same effect. The shear-water numbers on Lundy, for example, increased tenfold in the decade after it was declared rat-free,[11] although their slow path to sexual maturity generally makes the effect of these interventions a tricky and lengthy thing for scientists to measure.[12]

The concern initially had been that, once gone, the shear-waters would never come back, which they largely did. But it turns out that seabirds, as well as being highly philopatric (meaning that they return to the same breeding sites over and over again) are also great opportunists. When the new volcanic island of Surtsey rose from the North Atlantic waves in the early 1960s, it took only three years for guillemots and fulmars to establish colonies there, among the fresh volcanic fissures; 50 years later, it is host to at least fourteen breeding species.[13] These days, there is enough soil and vegetation on Surtsey for puffins to make burrows, which is perhaps only one step away from some pioneering Manx shearwaters. And the story of birds cheerfully breeding on an island that wasn't even there in the first half of the twentieth century should teach us a powerful lesson about the future, along the lines of new doors opening almost as readily as others close.

One of the positive changes between a hundred years ago and now is that, back then, we were killing our seabirds quite deliberately, whereas now it tends to be accidentally, a collateral result of the way we live. In 1913, W.H. Hudson could write, with heavy sarcasm: 'For in June and July the grouse and partridge and pheasant were not yet ready for the killing, and it was great fun in the meantime to have a few days with the gannets, terns, kittiwakes, guillemots and other auks.'* Driven kittiwake: you heard it here first. In those days, shearwaters were used for bait in lobster pots, and even ploughed into the ground as a form of organic manure. We have come a long way since then, something that we perhaps need to keep reminding ourselves, as we start to count what we no longer see, and treasure what we still have.

As we have seen, the Isle of Man still has thriving populations of brown rats, and is therefore devoid of shearwaters,

....

* *Adventures Among Birds*, W.H. Hudson (J.M. Dent & Sons, 1913). Hudson (1841–1922) often tramped the same Patagonian coastline as I had, when he was a boy, the son of English settlers. Founder member of the RSPB, he also has a town in Argentina named after him.

other than a toehold on the tiny neighbouring Calf of Man. Nature, despite what some like to attest, is often a zero sum game; where my species goes up, yours necessarily goes down. And just because seabird chicks happen to be more popular with the public than rats doesn't mean that there aren't committed conservationists who deeply regret the local exterminations of the latter.

Ultimately, there are three types of human being in the conservation business, starting with the 7.5 billion of us who spend our lives inadvertently creating and suffering from the shortages, the emissions, the warming oceans, the garbage and the trail of micro-plastics, to name but a few, as part of our daily, more or less well-intentioned lives. Then there are the few who actively make the problems worse, like the poachers of rhinoceroses or pangolins, serving that lucrative market of delusional sexual vanity; like the policy-makers who continue to reward and subsidise the extraction of fossil fuels or, for example, the French government when it issued licences for hunters to kill 6,000 Eurasian curlews in July 2019, even when faced with the evidence that 80%–90% of them had already disappeared from the whole region.* And finally there is the small number of dedicated scientists, field workers and conservationists who research, create and enable the policies, plans and actions to

....

* Wildfowl & Wetlands Trust report, August 2019. The saga is a classic illustration of the power of competing lobbying groups. First the powerful hunting lobby secured the licences (plus more for 30,000 red-listed turtle doves) in the face of all conservation logic and in contravention of the EU's Birds Directive; then the volume of the resulting outcry caused a welcome U-turn a month later. Moral: never give up.

sort out the mess. It is the Manx shearwater's intense good fortune to breed on islands that the latter group have largely kept free of the influences of the second one.

Predator populations are dictated by the current availability of prey, which, in turn, is largely governed by the ready availability of the right food. Sitting in the middle of that short chain, the shearwater finds itself, on the one hand, feeding in a sea of relative plenty, while, on the other, largely isolated from its most dedicated killer. They can cope with the gulls, skuas, eagles and ravens, because they have evolved alongside them and there are far, far more shearwaters than there are of these predators.*

That, as much as anything, is why they are doing pretty well, but just one pregnant rat could bring extinction to each island colony.

～┬～

You have to know what to look for but, if you do, a tiny emerald-green patch of sea thrift among the late summer heather tells the best story.

For there, above a small sea cliff overlooking the wild Atlantic on the northern coast of Tresco, is a hole in the ground with a slightly wider circumference than the base of a mug, and the important thing is that it wasn't there nine years ago. Or, if it was, it was empty or had a rabbit living in it.

---

* It is not for nothing that three out of four of those predator birds are on the endangered list (two red, one amber). The clever old raven, like his crow cousins, is on the increase.

On the runway into that hole is a tell-tale smearing of guano, and at its mouth a few pale breast feathers, hard evidence of recent night-time comings and goings that signal an active shearwater burrow below. Despite the fact that Tresco hasn't even been cleared of rats, the birds are not only here, but have colonised the island for the first time in living memory. Maybe there are only 40 pairs, and maybe it's still too soon to know if they will breed successfully, but it's 40 more than there were. And they are back on neighbouring Bryher, as well, and on other islands. Local conservationists think that they may well be 'overspill' birds from Lundy, that other cleared island a hundred miles or so up into the Bristol Channel.

I had gone down to the Isles of Scilly to see for myself the history, and the effect, of the rodent eradication scheme on St Agnes and Gugh. It is one thing laying down 1,000 baited traps of anticoagulant poison on an uninhabited island, but quite another to do so with a working population of 85 people living in the vicinity, as is the case on St Agnes. Admirably, at least two years was spent carefully bringing the islanders along with the project, consulting them at every turn, and not proceeding until everyone was in agreement that this was the right thing to do.[14] Even the tiny school ran occasional lessons on the relationship between rats and Manx shearwaters, and it was vital that the farming community worked with the eradication teams to deny the animals the rubbish that attracted them in the first place. The killing took place between October 2013 and March 2014, with no fewer than 1,000 'stations' of the poison laid out over the small islands, and nothing that wasn't a rat is thought to have died as collateral damage. The renaissance of breeding shearwaters has been spectacular, particularly so when you bear in mind that their single-egg strategy limits the speed at which their numbers can increase. Even now, the 'Rat on a Rat' observation campaign is still in full swing.

'Back in 2006, when the numbers were at their lowest, there were about 170 active burrows spread over six islands. That figure is now 523 over ten islands, probably quite a lot more, in fact.' Vickie Heaney, who for twenty years has been the seabird ecologist for the islands, has seen the population prosper, principally since St Agnes and neighbouring Gugh were cleared in 2013. 'But it's in stark contrast to what's happening to terns and kittiwakes,' she adds, in acknowledgement that the general direction of travel of our seabirds remains very much downwards. Her PhD work had been on terns, so she knew what she was talking about.

There are shearwaters breeding in only two places in England (Lundy Island is the other), so these are Britain's southernmost outriders of the species, uncrowded occupants of a rocky coastline, perhaps even queue-jumpers on the long southward journey to Argentina. Unless you knew exactly what you were looking for, and where, and when, you could visit Tresco a hundred times and still be utterly unaware of them. Because it's not until you are draining your final appreciative drink of the evening at the New Inn, a mile or so south, that the parents will start to return to the colony. And, as Skomer is a city, so Tresco is just a village; as Skomer rings out loudly with the bedlam noises of 10,000 birds at a time, here there are the optimistic cackles of just a few. Twenty years ago, English shearwaters were free-falling into a highly probable local extinction; now green shoots are emerging.

In many ways, Vickie is typical of the breed, scientific knowledge (a degree and PhD in Zoology from Oxford) mixing with endless nights camping on rainy shores, with a cheerful dollop of psychological know-how thrown in. 'When we were planning the clearance on St Agnes,' she says, 'we spent far more time over here discussing the residents' feelings than we ever did planning the actual work. As a result, not only did we end up with an island that was 100% supportive of what we were doing, but also a population that still actively help us monitor the situation today.'

We had crossed over to St Agnes and were playing back calls of male Manx shearwaters down the handful of burrows on the southern coast of the island to establish who inside might answer. Generally, censuses are done earlier in the season, between mid-May and mid-June, when it is most likely that an adult bird will be inside, but Vickie has much to cover and a limited number of hours in which to do it. She also needed to check the batteries on a couple of trail cameras among the boulders on the shore, trying to establish whether it was the local farm cats predating the newly-established colony of tiny storm petrels that nest deep within the crevices, or something else. Finally, she had to check the harmless wax bait inside a few black boxes scattered around the shoreline, specific teeth marks in which would disclose the dismal fact that the rats were back. They were untouched, as they have been for years, so all was well.

All done, we sat on the shore eating our sandwiches, the orange-gold and green of the lichens on the rocks playing off the yellow bird's-foot trefoil and the white-flecked blue of the sea. It was one of those moments that questions the sanity of the tarmac and concrete imperatives of our crowded lives. Nothing to watch but the sun bubbling in bright spots on the water, and nothing to hear but the cry of the gulls and the incessant rolling grumble of the sea caressing the rocks in front of us.

'What's the best bit of all this for you?' I asked, thinking for a moment that she might freeze-frame a scene like the one in front of us right now.

She thought for a moment, and then said with sudden decisiveness: 'Sometimes, if I'm up here at night in late August, I'll come across a chick at the mouth of its burrow, or even just outside it. No one really knows why. It's as if it's preparing itself for that long journey, testing the breeze, imprinting the map and star coordinates onto its brain. It sort of blows my mind to think what it has got coming up in a few weeks' time, where it will go, and how it will eventually find its way back.'

We looked out in silence over the infinity of water between us and the Bishop Rock lighthouse.

'We call them the star-gazers,' she said.*

I thought about the star-gazers for a while without having anything to add, apart from the unspoken conviction that it is largely because of the small, unnoticed army of people like Vickie that we have as many seabirds as we do. Sometimes these people are all that stands between a population and its extinction.

---

* A term first coined by Michael Brooke in his 1990 work, *The Manx Shearwater*.

A few days later, I watched the sunlit arc of the wake of RMV *Scillonian III* glittering back towards St Mary's. On both sides, a richness of birds was going about its business: stiff-winged fulmars quartering behind the boat on some off-chance of reward; gannets and gulls commuting between the islands, and everywhere small groups of Manx shearwaters bustling along down by the sea.

'Look at those seagulls,' said a young boy in sunglasses and an RSPB sweatshirt who might have been about the same age as I was for Bird Number 83 all those years ago. 'They're so cool.'

'Come away from the railings, Jack,' called his mother. 'You can see them any time.'

I thought about saying something, just one tiny element of what those 'seagulls' amounted to, because I knew deep down that every life has the occasional moment when the 'off' switch must be pressed to 'on'. But something in the mother's face suggested that the moment wasn't right.

At the same time, I started to feel the magnetic pull of north drawing me, before the season finished, back up to the islets and sea lochs where it had all started. North, not so much as a direction, but as 'a shifting affair, always relative, always going away from us ... moving out of reach and receding towards the polar night'.* North as part of wildness, and as an escape from the vanities and extravagances of the life I felt I was starting to leave behind. North, where I needed to find another boat.

There are goodbyes to be said, but it's not yet clear where, or to what, or to whom.

---

* *The Idea of North*, Peter Davidson (Reaktion Books, 2005).

12. THE CALL OF THE NORTH

August, Isle of Rum

The last time I saw my grandmother alive was down on the pierhead at Craignure after an autumn visit, a slightly stooped figure in jeans and a green quilted jacket, hair blown about in the wind.

She was waving to me, one arm aloft, as the ferry I was on prepared to reverse out into the Sound of Mull, the first frosts of winter gleaming on the Morvern hills on the mainland to our east. She was calling something to me which was drowned out by the boat's engines and the wind. I knew what it would be, though, as it was always the same. She had her little ceremonies, and the heartfelt goodbye was one of them.

'Haste ye back,' she would be shouting, invoking the old Gaelic farewell, 'and don't leave it too long.' And then I watched her striding off to her car, illegally parked in the space reserved for the emergency services. By the car, I saw her stop and talk animatedly to one of the ferry crew while he was supervising the loading of the last few vehicles, and I knew without hearing a word that what would have passed between them was her tip for the 3.20 at Market Rasen, and the evidence from *Timeform* that backed it up. It had been much on her mind at breakfast before we had left, and I was aware that the crewman was one of her partners in crime.

She was proud of my profession as a soldier, and rather delighted that I had chosen to spend my few days of leave from operations in Northern Ireland with her, rather than down south. I'd been given rock cakes, beer and a strong hug for the journey, already told what activities she had planned for my next visit. If I say now that I had a sharp presentiment about never seeing her again, it would be true, but only because it was a presentiment that I had felt on every departure for the last decade: the cocktail of heart pills and unfiltered cigarettes lying on her kitchen table simply didn't suggest to any of us that she would make old bones.

Two months later, my mother called me late one night in my battalion's operations room in Armagh City to say that my grandmother had died. She had been involved in a 'one vehicle crash' on her way back down the single-track road through Glen More after Sunday lunch with one of her widow friends. Quite how my mother had got through to me was unclear, as our time under the red glow of the Ops room light was supposed to be given to intercepting terrorist atrocities, not receiving calls from concerned relatives. Also, it must have been an especially difficult call for her to make; she would have been more than aware that the love her mother had largely denied her own daughters, had been lavished instead in abundance on the next generation down, and that our two sadnesses were probably therefore fated to be subtly different ones.

For a while after I had put the receiver down, I said nothing, just staring instead at the large operational map of South Armagh that covered the wall in front of me. Red, blue and green pins marked the villages where we patrolled, and we had been shifting them around for the following day's activities when the call had come in. I shut my mind off completely to the news I had just heard, and worked instead on the patrol plan and the helicopter tasking sheet for tomorrow. 'Not now,' I thought to myself every time her face swam into view that evening. 'Please, not now.' It was a technique that I used on and off for the next 30 years.

The inference was that she had gone to sleep at the wheel and that, once she had ascertained from the Forestry Commission man who first tended her at the scene that her new dog was dead and not injured, gave up any further ambition for life herself. 'It's a blessing, really,' said a distant cousin rather too cheerfully, after her funeral service. While true in part, it was not really what I wanted to hear. Equally, we all knew in our hearts that she would have made an unconvincing sweet old grandmother in some care home, and an unhappy exile from the wild world that sustained her. It has to be said that any care home with her in it would quickly have had its own card school, betting ring, investment club and debating chamber.

On the gravestone in the beautiful churchyard where she was laid was inscribed a tiny songbird. It was striking, and it was simple, but nonetheless I would have given her a seabird, if only as a metaphor for the distance that she had covered in her life.

The house was sold and the physical ties broken. All those firm reference points of our time there – the garden, the heather, the games of canasta, the seals, the Bunessan show, the green stones, the islanders, the ragwort, and the serried ranks of bird-life – were rewound like an old tape spool, traded off for future memories in the rush to move on. By the time there was a collective idea among the cousins that we might want to club together and keep it, the little whitewashed cottage had become someone else's rightful dream, and it was too late.

From time to time, I heard their name mentioned – here as an indie rock band, there as a boat company – but, for a quarter of a century, I could never quite bring myself to go and find those shearwaters again. They had flown off with her in the Glen, and with them, as it turned out, the last tangible shards of my childhood.

After the long drive north from Penzance, and for the next two weeks as the parched hayfields of late summer started to hint of an autumn soon to come, it was all boats.

And, because it was all boats, the shearwaters, so often the unreachable lantern on the moor in my last twelve months, now began to dominate my days. It seemed that they were

everywhere, that no patch of sea was without those dark, pur-
poseful, stiff-winged shapes shearing and soaring their way
between the waves and the other seabirds.

There were certainly easier ways of getting myself to those
plentiful waters off Rum, but then there were certainly easier
summers in which to do it. The Welsh islands were still closed
due to the lockdown, which meant that I had to abandon T72B
until some possible time in the future, but most of the Scottish
islands were open, or at least they were if you could get to
them. The problem with getting to them was that the ferries
were only taking about 25% of their usual passengers, and
often not even that, which meant that there was a very good
chance of my staring over the sea from Mallaig jealously imag-
ining life back on the islands without actually ever reaching
them. Plus, it turned out that many of the owners of the hotels
and bed and breakfast cottages had decided not to open at all,
meaning that I needed a tent, and a car that I could sleep in
if I didn't fancy pitching the tent. I also needed to find people
with boats, specifically boats that were not part-owned by the
Scottish government.

Crossing the little Corran Ferry with its left-hand turn
into 'the heart of Gaeldom on earth',[1] I finalised a plan that,
even by my standards, was contrived beyond logic. In an echo
of Argentina, it involved an extensive knowledge and use of
degrees of separation, in which friend A (in my village), had an
old schoolfriend (B) on the Isle of Muck, with a brother-in-law
(C) with a seaworthy boat which, happily, would be available
for a couple of days. Then cousin D in Argyll had a former
workmate (E) on Mull who had a friend (F) in Ardnamurchan,

who would be happy to let me stay with her at the end of my long journey. And finally, ex-colleague G, who happened to be pottering down the western isles in a sailing boat at the time, quickly saw the potential amusement in diverting, collecting me, and then taking me on to an unspecified 'somewhere else' afterwards. 'Where the wind takes us?' he asked, when I was unable to tell him exactly where I wanted to go, and I agreed that this would be a suitable basis for the second part of the trip. There are, after all, 35 islands in the Inner Hebrides, and the current direction of the wind is a particularly appropriate device by which to decide which of them to visit, if you are not in any rush.

And so, having driven almost the full length of Britain, I abandoned the car in the little crofting community of Kilchoan and hiked across the Ardnamurchan Peninsula (fulfilling another tiny childhood ambition) to the even smaller crofting community of Sanna, where I had arranged to meet C on the beach. A few hardy kayakers looked over in confusion as I took my backpack off, laid it on the sand and waved energetically at the occupants of a single fishing boat anchored out in the swell beyond the rocks. I then watched as a small rubber dinghy was launched and headed over towards the shore. This crafting of a new adventure out of unusual circumstances felt cheerfully in tune with the closing stages of my search. Being picked up from a strange and remote beach in a rubber dinghy and heading out into the sea with no particular plan was exactly the kind of thing I wished I could have done in Argentina all those months before. We transhipped to the bigger craft beyond the rocks, and then headed over to Muck where we waited for the right conditions to get out to the mass rafts of shearwaters off Rum, seven or eight miles to the north. If it was all slightly more complex than it strictly needed to be, it had the unassailable advantage of being an adventure, itself more than enough justification for the whole thing.

Seabirds, islands and wilderness, together, are a cocktail that almost always produces adventure. That old 1917 penny deep in a side pocket of my rucksack made it a racing certainty.

—⁓—

Rafting is basically the shearwaters' equivalent of a waiting room.

The adult birds spend the majority of daylight hours foraging, sometimes close to the shore and sometimes far out to sea, driven as always by hunger, habit and the powerful scent of food. At the back end of the season, these foraging trips have the additional pull of urgency, as it is now only a week or two until the first birds will fly south again, at which point the next meal that a chick will get will have to be self-service. Towards the end of the afternoon, they will start to gather on the sea close to their colonies, growing in number and drifting slowly towards to the shore as they wait for complete darkness to allow them to come up in safety and feed their chicks.

This gathering is as spectacular an expression of the sheer weight of their population as you will ever find, hence why I had come up to see it. It is the quiet counterpoint of the bedlam nights high above and, in its own way, one of the most gently impressive wildlife events that Britain has to offer. The longer the afternoon and evening wear on, the more of them turn up from out in their foraging grounds until the whole surface of the sea is taken up with dark-backed birds floating around. There is evidently a social element to it all and, while feeding from rafts is not infrequent, it is not the main point of the exercise. Relationships are established, courtship may be inaugurated and petty quarrels enacted, just like they are in any waiting room. The time at rest on the water also provides an opportunity to preen, something that any seabird needs to do regularly in order to keep waterproof and airworthy. When the weather is calm, so are they, but when the wind is blowing, they will restlessly rise into and fall from the air as if trying to hold a position that is important to them. Research has indicated that this is probably the case, by establishing that the location of the raft is governed principally by the location of the colony that the individual bird comes from (meaning it is as close as possible), and by the fact that the tendency of the raft is to approach the shore the nearer it gets to complete darkness.[2] The primary aim of it all, of course, is to arrive at the burrow after the last predator has gone, in some giant natural game of grandmother's footsteps.

Whereas the previous year I had generally been happy to rely on the Caledonian MacBrayne ferry to provide my opportunities to observe shearwaters at sea, I realised that asking the captain to stop the boat every ten minutes so that I could watch things at my leisure was not an option for this trip. A £4.00 ferry ticket was an attractively low cost of research, but it carried with it a depressingly high chance of seeing nothing.

Thus, early one breathless Saturday evening, I slipped out of Port Mòr harbour on the Isle of Muck, with brother-in-law

C, who was called Colin. Colin had been asked to do many things in his time as a boatman, and from the start he hid very well the probability that sitting in the middle of a large patch of resting seabirds, doing nothing much more than just watching them for the best part of an evening wasn't one of them. After asking the advice of the warden on Rum, who often took boat trips out in the evenings to see these rafts herself, we picked an area of sea between the north tip of the island of Eigg and Hallival on Rum; wondering, as I often did, whether this would be one of the nights that the birds didn't bother, or just decided to go somewhere else.

At 5.15pm, we noticed the first 50 or so birds come in, their profiles black against the blue of the Cuillin Hills on Skye. Settling only for the briefest of moments, they kept rising and falling off the surface of the sea in invisible ropes of movement, skittish in the light breeze, while more and more joined them. An hour later, the main congregation had moved further north to the narrowest part of the channel between Eigg and Rum, and had grown to around 500 birds. For a moment or two, we watched in rapt attention as three minke whales breached repeatedly as they described a semi-circular arc through the centre of the raft, each breaking of the surface pushing the birds a few feet back up into the sky for a second or two.

'Wasn't expecting that,' said Colin quietly.

All the while, more and more birds were flying in to join the raft, landing inelegantly on the water with a paddle of feet and a slight forwards head butt, and then settling in for the evening in increasing serenity. Early on, I tried to count them, but it was hopeless: the raft we were in the middle of was simply a small one within a far, far larger grouping that spread across more than a square mile of sea, an army of black and white birds bobbing up and down on the water. To say that there were 10,000 was, if unscientific, not unthinkable, given that numbers of 30,000 or more have been recorded in the same area in recent times. And still they came, their quiet calls drowned by the grumbling of the ubiquitous guillemots and the urgent, seaward honks of the bottle-shaped, night-time greylag geese flighting out of Rum; still they came, back from the fishing grounds off Mull and Skye, off Tiree and Lewis, each a returner from the dawn diaspora to the guts of the mountains high above them.

This was the very antithesis of the thumps, whirrs and bedlam noises that would take place 2,000 feet above us in a few hours' time. It amused me to think that Tim Guilford and Ollie Padget had arrived on Rum that very afternoon, and would even now be settling back into the hut for a week of research. *My* birds would become *their* birds soon enough, after the last of the light had leaked away from the sky, and the last threatening buzzard had drifted back down to its roost in the wood behind Kinloch village.

And still they came, the evening opportunists from local waters and the late-comers from out in the Irish Sea, until the whole surface of the sea around us was pock-marked with their darkening shapes. Wherever I looked, there were shearwaters, more by far in one place than I had seen in the last twelve months put together. Here, finally, was the physical evidence of the numerical claims; here in the only setting in which this secretive, intrepid bird makes it easy to be followed. In a way, it made laughable the lengths I had gone to in Patagonia just to find a couple, or the biblical wet that I had put my body through in West Cork to get a glimpse of a bird or two in the act of arriving. But only in a way: all creatures are a product of everything they do and everywhere they go, and the deal I had made with myself a year ago in the same bit of water was that I would follow them as faithfully as I possibly could. I was beginning to feel that I had just about been true to my word.

Every now and again, one would ascend, paddling its feet like a swan rising from the Thames, and then fly a few yards to settle down in other company. Then, as the red sky drained slowly out over Canna on the western horizon, two fins marked where a basking shark was making its slow way through a small area of the raft, a creature 10,000 times the weight of each of the shearwaters around it, but absorbing in the plankton it harvested a food source that might be 10,000 times smaller than the pilchards the birds had been feeding on an hour ago.

'Wasn't expecting that either,' said Colin. 'That's the first one this year.'

It was one of those evenings.

~~~

'So what *is* going on under there?' asked Wendy, nodding at the water that *Mikara* was passing through. 'We can see what the birds are doing above and on the water, but what about below it?'

It was a couple of days later, mirror-calm, and we were trying to make our slow way westwards under sail through the stillness, across the channel from Muck to Coll. My friends Hugh and Wendy had collected me from the Isle of Muck and we were doing precisely what Hugh and I had agreed, just seeing where the wind blew us, what little of it there was. Behind us was a pattern of islands, stretching into the infinity of beyond, each a paler shade of blue than the one in front, in an almost unreasonable display of beauty. Another day, another boat, and another world of guillemots patiently teaching their chicks to fish; a world where the loudest noise was of the tireless rhythmic breath of the ebb tide on the nearby shingle shore. A few single shearwaters flew around, but most of them were out at sea with the fresher breezes.

I thought about those hidden dimensions that were blurred secrets from our unadapted eyes. Sometimes, if it was crystal clear, you could see for yourself the way the different birds propelled themselves through the water, but anything further away than a few feet remained a mystery.

'Well, I suppose you would start with those ones, over there,' I said, pointing at a couple of fulmars on the water between us and the tip of Coll. 'They won't dive, but will mainly scavenge what they need off the surface. Then, a few metres down, maybe seven or eight, at the bottom of their duck dive, shearwaters might be chasing tiny pilchards back up towards the surface, pushing themselves through the water with their feet. They are built to go deeper, like all marine birds, but they tend not to.'

Warming to my subject, I mentioned that, passing below the shearwaters, a mass of bubbles might show us the end point of a gannet's 60 mph dive, where it starts to pursue what it first saw from 30 metres up; and crossing it, in the other direction, a cormorant might be snaking its way through the water. Further down still, maybe 20 or 30 metres, we might see a puffin 'flying' by on its short, stubby wings, five or six sand eels gripped to the roof of her mouth, held into place by a rasping tongue, and allowing her to catch more as she goes along.

Being boring about seabirds was something I could do without breaking into a sweat, so I went on: 'Down at 50 metres or so, you might find a razorbill catching a small cod as he swims his way through the melee of sprats and herrings; he'll eat it up as he's going along. And down we go, till the bubbling dots of sunshine on the surface are a mere impressionist memory in the darkness, and there, as deep as the spire of Salisbury Cathedral is high, we might be lucky enough to find a lone guillemot flying her way through the lowest shoals of sprats to bring a meal back up to some cliff over there by Ardnamurchan lighthouse.* A million seabirds will take a very large tonnage of fish from the sea over the course of a summer.'

Of course, it was all a flight of the imagination, but the telling of it re-awoke in me a little frisson of the childlike amazement I had felt all those months earlier when I was starting on my journey of discovery. Before I had begun to let

....

* Just to put this in context, on July 19th 2006, an emperor penguin was recorded as diving to 564 metres (1,850 feet) off eastern Antarctica, the deepest ever recorded bird dive (*Guinness Book of World Records*). The elephant seal knocks it cold with a recorded 100-minute dive down to 2,388 metres (7,835 feet), which is over a mile and a half.

science peel back the layers of unknowing, I could never have imagined answering Wendy's question. Now, I was just sitting there, innocently hoping that she might ask more.

As I lay on my bunk that evening to the sound of the tide quietly slapping its fingers against the hull of *Mikara* below me, too energised by the last few days to sleep, I turned to the question of exactly how and where my year should end.

I had now been following Manx shearwaters, just as I had promised myself I would, for almost twelve months. I had watched them in two different hemispheres and on countless islands in rain, sunshine, storm, calm, darkness and light. I had observed them on land and sea, in the air, on the water, on the ground, and down inside it. Sometimes, I had just completely failed to find them. Sometimes, where I had found them, I had held them, weighed them and ringed them. I had questioned professors, wardens, PhD students, volunteers and undergraduates. I had sat poring over books in libraries, museums and zoology faculties. I had read what seemed to be every scientific paper ever written on them, and an unhealthy quantity of general books about seabirds besides. I was getting to the point that I had as wide a general knowledge about this one bird as anyone out there. My close friends were beginning to think my life was becoming uncomfortably single-issue. They were right. But perhaps it wasn't just the single-tracked obsession they thought it was.

I was beginning to understand with greater clarity each day that this little story needed to finish where it had started almost 50 years ago, when that eleven-year-old boy noticed an unfamiliar bird shearing the waters behind a boat he was on, and Bird Number 83 flew into his life for the first time, 17,890 days ago.

From the research point of view, there was no need for me to head back to Lunga, that little island off Mull with its insignificant shearwater colony. I knew what I would find there, and it would add nothing to the science: a small, outlying colony of shearwaters doing their own thing. But I also knew that it was about much more than a particular bird. It was about the person and the island that had given them to me in the first place. The journey needed to come to an end in the same ocean where it had started, rather than on a train pulling in to King's Cross. More keenly than ever, I felt the pull of the basalt columns of Staffa, of the pink granite rocks of the Ross of Mull, and of a little white cottage perched on a low hill above a sea inlet.

13. JOURNEY'S END

August/September, Isle of Mull

··

*Let your joy be in your journey,
not in some distant goal.*
TIM COOK

··

Happily, I was alone as I fell unceremoniously out of the boot of my small estate car by the side of Loch Scridain at sunrise.

I had been trying to carry out a number of mutually incompatible housekeeping actions while perched in a sleeping bag on the edge of the boot where I had been sleeping since the midges had driven me from the tent a few hours before, and it hadn't worked. No damage worse than indignity was done, and for a second or two I just lay on the side of the road like a giant green 60-year-old larva, and reflected, as I looked up at Ben More, with growing contentment about the last few days.

They say that you should never go back, I thought, but they are so wrong. You must go back. Reunited with my car at Kilchoan, I had taken the little ferry over to Tobermory the evening before and landed once again on Mull, a self-exile returning quietly to a familiar shore. If I had a plan, it was a sketchy one, a soft-focus reworking of decades-old routines that would lead me inexorably down towards Fionnphort, and the waters of memory beyond. Beyond involving another boat or two at some stage, it was a plan that would just go, like *Mikara*, wherever the wind happened to blow it. The 1917 penny had moved from the backpack to the pocket of my jeans, just as the Ordnance Survey map on the passenger seat of the car was swapped from Sheet 39 (*Rum, Eigg and Muck*) to Sheet 48 (*Iona and West Mull*).

I looked back up at Ben More, crouching lion-like over the Ross of Mull in the half light, and decided on a whim that the day should formally start with breakfast on top of it, even if it were to be a breakfast whose nutritional value would be limited to a half packet of slightly stale digestive biscuits from the glove compartment of my car, some fruit pastilles and a couple of bottles of water. I drove round to the north side of the mountain to take advantage of the short, dry but relentless ascent from Loch na Keal, and was pleasantly surprised by the old soldier's muscle memory that made me plod steadily on upwards, never really stopping, never looking backwards at the view, until I was at the summit cairn a couple of hours later. If I was expecting to hear forgotten voices up there, I didn't; the only sounds were the faint cascading of the burn far below, and the pulses of breeze that blew through the short-cropped tufts of the lichens and mosses of the summit plateau. I could see all the way down the twenty-mile peninsula of the Ross of Mull and clearly make out Iona at the end, and everything that lay between. Especially what lay in between.

Back at sea level, I abandoned the car a mile or so short of Bunessan, sensing that this part of my past was something that needed to be walked through, not driven over; lingered in and not passed by at speed. I am not sure what I was expecting to see or not see but, whatever it was, it was all still there. The backdrop of the Burg over Loch Scridain when I looked over my right shoulder, with its sharply defined layers that marked out prehistoric volcanic activity; the little white stone mile posts that counted down the distance to Iona; the shelduck and herons out on the shores of the loch and the quiet highland cattle chewing the cud on the side of the road. It had become a hot, clear day, and I was glad that I had taken the little day pack with some water, rather than something heavier.

I reached the hill above Bunessan, the village where we used to do 'the messages', as my grandmother called the daily shopping, and stopped to look at the unchanged agricultural showground by the village school where she had won, year after year, the prize for the basket of mixed vegetables and much else besides. Maybe right then I heard some of the old voices, and maybe I could see in my mind's eye the little pens with the black-faced ewes waiting to be shown, and the marquee where Mary Hardwick's plate of three drop scones scooped the cup the year that Red Alligator took the Grand National. Maybe I could hear the faint echo of the bagpipes and see the kilted girls doing their sword-dance. Maybe my heart rate increased imperceptibly as I crested the hill and saw for the first time in 33 years the hill directly opposite Loch Caol, not because I feared being there, but because I feared that simply too much time had gone by for – well, for I knew not what.

As it turned out, down in Bayview Stores, they remembered me, even if it was primarily as a grandson.

'Oh, we still miss her terribly,' said Glen, now in his eighties. 'They don't make them like that any more.' The cliché was true enough, as they never do, and it worked with me because it was what I wanted to hear. I bought myself an apple and some more digestives, in celebration of a homecoming, and paid for them at the same Formica table where the Dutchman had told me about the black guillemots nearly 50 years before. Then I set off again to walk the last three miles. Past the ceilidh blockhouse where I discovered one teenage summer that first sharp feeling of painful and unrequited lust for the daughter of a local crab fisherman; past the pier with its lobster creels and blue plastic fish-boxes, where the evening shellfish were landed; past the tiny graveyard on the hill with its view out into the infinity of the Treshnish Islands and beyond. My memories were gradually returning in their proper, unimagined order.

On I walked. Past Tiraghoil Farm, where we used to pick up the creamy milk every morning, still warm in its small churn; off the road and past the granite gatepost where I scraped the side of my car the first time I was old enough to drive to Mull on my own; past the loch head where I once stole a gimballed brass compass from the cockpit of a wrecked trawler out on the mud; past the little wood on the left where my sister and I endlessly cleared paths in the bracken with sickles and scythes;

past the first knockings of the uneven lawn where I used to curse the granite rocks as I pushed the hopeless mower round; past the rope swing where my grandmother had once broken her hip testing out a new height setting. And then, then there was nothing else to pass. I was back.

For an instant, I just stood and looked around. Down south, where housing estates and unlovely retail parks could rise from a field of weeds in a matter of months, I had become inured to the endless bricking over of our world. Here, where the financial mathematics didn't work so well for the joyless developers, there were few new houses, no big alterations to the topography, and a quiet comfort seeped back into my bones after my nervous journey through the glen the previous evening. What I had most worried about had not happened, and the magic of the place that had been wired into my memory from all those childhood visits was intact. I had no right to be possessive of the spirit of this place I had no claim on, but I could not help what I thought.

Out from the deepest canyons of my brain, unbidden, tumbled the now freed sensations of my childhood. I could hear again the hollow echo of the black and white tiles in the kitchen, could feel the rough texture under my bare feet of the rush matting that led down the dark corridor to the sitting room where, a lifetime ago, I had sought out those books on shearwaters. I could feel on my lips the rim of the smoked plastic beaker full of lime cordial, and taste the porridge fresh from its overnighting on the little range in the *bain marie*; I could smell the ragwort on tired fingers, the mackerel fried in oatmeal, Elliman's Embrocation in the peaty bathtub under the framed copy of *Desiderata* on which my grandmother's sister had underlined the words 'Beyond a wholesome discipline, be gentle with yourself'. A beam of dusty daylight shone onto things that had lain undisturbed for a third of a century, as if someone had bottled the essence of a childhood and passed it out of the window to me.

The old heavy creosoted gate had gone, in favour of a modern, lightweight one which swung easily on its hinges when I unhooked its catch, and the thick layer of pebbles that I had cursed a thousand times as I pushed wheelbarrows of seaweed across them had been replaced by a concrete path. Shrubs had appeared where there were no shrubs before, and of the giant vegetable garden there was no sign. The huge log pile along the granite wall, whose constant refilling was part of the price we paid for our accommodation, had gone too, and I noticed double-glazing in the windows. Where there had been a ramshackle collection of sheds and caravans along the southern boundary, there was now just a fuchsia hedge, and in that instant I understood.

This was no longer my house in anything but memory, and memory was where it belonged. The only real point was that this was all right, and the natural order of things. The people who had bought it back in 1986 had actually lived in it longer than my grandmother had, and had made it theirs. Judging them for making it more comfortable, tidier and less wild was unfair and unrealistic; it was simply putting the museum of my childhood dreams above the needs of real people. I looked up at a lesser black-backed inheritor of Laurel and Hardy on the chimney and pulled the knocker back to see if anyone was home, but then stopped before I struck it back down again. What had suddenly halted me in my tracks was the realisation that I no longer needed to be there. The spell, if there had been one, was broken, and I had been given permission to move on.

Thirty-four years had gone past since that telephone call of my mother's, and it had taken a shearwater to bring me back again. Quietly, I lowered the knocker back to its housing, looked around one more time and started to walk quickly away.

Mark Jardine was the inheritor of Callum.

He had to be, for me at least, because he ran sea trips out of Fionnphort, just as Callum had done all those years before. So did others, to be fair, but Mark's boat was a 60-foot Danish gaff ketch, a *haikutter*, whose graceful lines and red sails had rather taken my fancy when I looked at his website.[1] Also, something suggested to me that the last shearwaters of my summer should be seen against the soundscape of gently flapping canvas and not the crude chug of a diesel engine.

'I've a space for you in the boat tomorrow,' he had said when I called. 'We're going out to Lunga if the weather allows.' *If the weather allows* – those four words that define life on the island fringes.

The following morning I arrived in Fionnphort legally, and on foot, rather than illegally at the wheel of a Land Rover, as I had all those years ago. While I waited for Mark to come over from Iona with the *Birthe Marie*, I watched the comings and goings onto the little ferry boat that plies the sound between the two islands, and had a quick go at the crossword from the previous day's *Times*. 'Where a rat's destroyed a bird (10 letters)', ran the clue of 7 down,* delivering on my last day out in the field one of the few real coincidences of my journey.

Mark turned out to be as quietly cheerful as Callum had been quietly lugubrious, and he was amused by the historical symmetry of my two visits.

'You'll not see too many changes since then, out here,' he said, almost by way of reassurance, as we made our way through the Bull Hole channel. 'Maybe they still had grazing on Lunga and Dutchman's Cap back then, but that'll be about it.'

I sat on my own in the bows as we turned to starboard off the little village of Kintra, and headed once again north towards Staffa. On that day with Callum, I thought to myself, I had been a slightly grubby boy with a Collins bird book, a minuscule diary and a tiny, blunt pencil that even my small schoolboy fingers were too big to write properly with; right now, the circumstances of my last few days and nights had ensured that I was a slightly grubby 60-year-old, once again with a Collins bird book, albeit a newer one, and paper and pencil with which I was once again scrawling things down against the occasional shudders of the waves. It was just in the bulk, the beard and the glasses that the spiralling years were perhaps reflected, and I found myself thinking of a comment of Nelson Mandela that I had once jotted down in the commonplace book I had been given in that cottage only four miles from here: 'There is

....

* 'Shearwater', for those who really can't do cryptic crosswords.

nothing like returning to a place that remains unchanged,' he had said, 'to find the ways in which you yourself have altered.'

I knew I'd find a shearwater, so I wasn't even looking for one; not consciously at least.

But there it was, soon enough. To be precise, there they were. In keeping with the last few weeks, hundreds of Manx shearwaters were darting across the waves, at more or less the exact point where I had seen Bird Number 83, 49 years before. There were far too many for them to have come solely from Lunga, so they must have drifted over from the hills of Rum, pushing out through the growing halo of shortage in its surrounding seas until they found the forage they needed.

'What are those birds?' asked one of my fellow passengers, following the glissades of movement out over the stern of the boat.

'Don't start,' I thought to myself. 'Don't even go there.' The instruction was to me, not to her. I told her its name, and saw her tick it off in her field guide.

Silhouetted against the Dutchman's Cap on the near horizon, on they came, carving their paths swiftly out of the middle distance, one, then two, then five, then twenty, travellers from the north fishing the plentiful waters off Mull, black and white against the battleship grey of the sea. In and out they flew between the brilliant white gannets and over the flocks of kittiwakes sitting expectantly on the sea. At the speeds they were travelling, it was hard to see how they could catch the snatch of sulphide in the wind that would lead them to a meal, but they could. As if to prove this, from time to time one would stall and drop to the sea with an ungainly flop that somehow belied its claim to be a supreme flier. These were the close-feeding birds from the colony, the ones who had just made a 30-mile hop to a neighbouring sea rather than a journey of ten times that length out into the near Atlantic; in consequence, the food would be less digested by the time it got to the chick,[2] and the bird itself would be one of those I'd seen back at the raft. All those nights of cross-billed feeding down in the burrows over the last two months may not be pretty, but it is mighty effective, and that waiting chick is now substantially heavier than either of its parents.

On Lunga, I ate my sandwich alone in the tiny colony on a clifftop, watching the fulmars riding the updraughts within a few feet of me. With my binoculars, I could see shearwaters still darting around in the area between Lunga and Calgary Bay, and I reflected on their coming journey. Soon they would be gone, driven perhaps by a sense of approaching hunger, or simply by *zugunruhe*, that familiar sense of restlessness initiated by the shortening days and some primal understanding that now is quite simply the time to go. Back in the burrow, the chick will be on its own for the next ten days, until its own restlessness and hunger start to drive it up to the entrance deep in the night, to look around, flap its wings and gaze at the stars. It may wander as far as 50 metres from the burrow on these occasions, but it will always return – even though there is no longer any reason for it to go back to the exact burrow in which it was born – to complete the transformation between defenceless, downy chick and effective master navigator.

All around me was the essence of the bird I had once only dreamed about: the moss-fronted burrow on the high sea cliff, guano on the earth with feathers on the grass, the little red fishing boat, the wind and the white-backed waves. A year ago, I might have looked into the infinity of the ocean to our west and seen it as something almost of regret, separating me from the natural world it hid, but no longer. So long as ocean birds need to come to shore to breed, we can see them, be with them, learn from them and, if we are researchers, even touch them, so long as we do it to the rhythm of their season, and do the best we can to create a world that will once again sustain them. Those little black and white birds out there – the inheritors of Bird Number 83 – were slowly increasing in number year after year. If they could do that with all the rats, cats, gulls, skuas, buzzards, lights, wind turbines, disease, long-line fishermen, storms and God knows what else that was routinely deployed against them, just think what they could do – what all the other pelagic birds could do for that matter – if we actually started mending the bits of their world that we have broken.

Stripped of all the attendant science and complexity that I had thrown its way in the last year, the shearwater remained a simple metaphor for the act of going beyond the horizon.

Behind me, some of the rocks had the tell-tale vertical scratch marks that indicate where a previous generation of birds had used their hooked beaks – that 'fifth limb' that Lockley talked about – to drag themselves up a little higher, to where the wind under their wings would be that little bit stronger and the ascent into the air that little bit easier. If I sat there for long enough, I would see it for myself again, as I had on Skomer almost a year ago when T72 dragged herself as high as she reasonably could, and then simply flew off into the darkness above us. But since then, I had gone the full year with them, and instinctively I knew that now was the right time to leave them alone. It was high time for *Pardela* Man, as the hostel owner had briefly referred to me that morning last November in Puerto Pirámides, to return to his own colony, mow the lawn and leave the birds be.

'All done,' I texted home. 'Back late tomorrow.'

~⌇~

It was getting on for evening when Mark started to pull down the sails as we made our way towards the first of the skerries that protect the end of Iona from the worst of the weather when it comes from the north.

Sleepy with the previous day's exertions and the slight rhythmic pitching of the *Birthe Marie*, I had dozed off from time to time on the two-hour journey back from Lunga, watching the passing scene intermittently through the geometric gaps created by her various ropes, sheets and halyards. Every time I opened my eyes, it seemed, there was a shearwater out there in reasonable proximity to the boat. If I dreamed, it wasn't about much, or for long; more a subtle and shallow changing of levels between consciousness and oblivion, like a salmon on its run up the river. All I could think about, all that really seemed to matter, was the sense of fulfilment and bereavement that the end of a long journey always brings.

'Did you get what you came for?' asked Mark, as he came to the bow of the boat to deploy the fenders for our imminent arrival at Fionnphort.

'I did. And thank you. It was great.' There wasn't a lot more that I could say.

Leaning as far as I dared over the side, I trailed my hand for a moment in the passing wash of the boat, feeling the alternating cold and warm pulses of the wine-dark water cooling my blood. Gradually, I unclenched my half-disembodied fist and stared as the sunlight caught briefly on the dull metal of an old copper coin, refracting like a tiny mackerel weight as it made its slow way down to the sea bed 200 feet below. I watched the coin until it had been fully absorbed into the darkness, then looked up and astern of the *Birthe Marie*.

There, off the port quarter, just as they had been nearly 50 years ago, were three birds shearing their way westward towards the dipping sun, Argentina and a new tomorrow.

AFTERWORD

Some time ago, I read an online article under the headline 'Turtle dove hurtles towards extinction'.

I love turtle doves, and so read it with a due sense of foreboding. However, as the piece progressed, it became clearer and clearer that, so long as you weren't a turtle dove, it was a good news story wrapped under an attention-grabbing bad news headline. When all is said and done, current farm stewardship policies have seen a reversal of many of the hideous declines in farmland bird species since the turn of the century. Skylarks, corn buntings, reed buntings and linnets are all up, ditto the goldcrest, pied flycatcher and chiffchaff. In fact, 32% of farmland species had shown an increase, compared to 42% whose populations were stable and 26% that had declined.

In a world of catastrophic natural decline, these modest figures, which my daily dog walks had already prompted me to think might be true, stood out as a shining beacon of hope, and hope is what activists need. If I hadn't happened to have been interested in turtle doves, I would have just noted the headline, added it to the other depressing headlines I saw, and headed off to do my day's work.

More importantly, I would have further convinced myself of humanity's inability to influence for the good any of the destruction we have wrought. And, being convinced that I couldn't influence, I wouldn't even try to. Far from joining the little platoon of people – politicians included – who are working to get something done, I would have melted back into the ranks of the vast army of folk who just think it's a done deal.

For sure, the fundamental challenge for our seabirds is that mankind is simply producing habitat and environmental changes at a far greater rate than the birds can adapt to them, changes that underpin the fragility that has seen between two thirds and three quarters of them disappear in roughly the time since I had stared off the back of Callum's boat as an eleven-year-old boy. Take industrial fishing. The evidence is that seabirds are now eating smaller and smaller prey, from further and further down the food chain, because the larger fish are no longer available to them.[1] Or plastics. Research suggests that 90% of the world's seabirds have plastic in their stomachs, which can lead to starvation, toxicity and bowel obstruction, not to mention the effect on a chick that is inadvertently fed it. Only 2% of the world's oceans are in any sense protected, (the figure for dry land is 15%), and less than half of what is protected is actually closed to fishing.[2] But these things can change, and some already are.

Our Age of the Sixth Extinction, driven as it has been by our own activities, and coloured as it is by our own species' sense of self-importance, is one that is hard for us to talk about dispassionately, and yet we must. We are simply the adult version of the children we once were; and children, as every child psychologist will tell you, need more encouragement in their lives than criticism. If all we ever hear is the doomsday sound of future extinctions knocking on our skulls, we will eventually come to accept that this is how it will all end. We will not celebrate the myriad little victories all around us, which will eventually become meaningful staging posts in the war against what we have done. Have you read any articles about the depleted ozone layer since we successfully started to reverse it, or since we heard that it would probably be fully patched by 2040? Me neither. Sadly, good news stories don't sell papers, and they don't help fundraisers.

Just because we are in deep ecological danger, and we really are, it doesn't follow that we should ignore the lifelines being lowered to us. This is not a mandate for some saccharine denial of what is going on out there, but an argument for a true sense of balance.

During my shearwater year, I learned afresh how to look at nature. For sure, I kept the childlike fascination that took me to birds in the first place as a young boy in the 1960s and 1970s, and the marvelling in a creature the size and weight of a paperback book that would not touch solid ground for maybe three years. But I also started to notice the scientists at work in the background on the breeding islands, and the long-term reductions in bycatch from the changes in long-line fishing; I saw the beneficial effects of fishing quota policy, and the population explosions that followed island restoration pro-grammes; I saw the effects of the National Park movement, and of Britain's 89 marine conservation zones. And I began to detect an outbreak of joined-up thinking that just might start to reverse seven decades of decline in our seabird biomass. Each time I crossed to an island, or climbed into a mountain colony, I was struck not by how little people were already doing, but how much.

Knowledge, policy and activism, that's what makes things happen, as initiated by scientists, politicians and conservationists respectively.

Right now, the Manx shearwater is a lucky bird, and my hope for this book is that it helps us all celebrate that.

RTMG
West Sussex, September 2020

SOMETHING VERY SIMPLE YOU CAN DO FOR SHEARWATERS

While the Manx shearwater has a stable, even an increasing population, the closely related Balearic shearwater is hurtling towards extinction, with the population shrinking by about 14% each year.

This is happening for all the sadly 'normal' reasons (bycatch from fishing, warming oceans, shrinking breeding grounds and human disturbance), and it is vital to take effective steps to protect and support those left. This happens only with the help of rigorous and surprisingly expensive research.

In 2015, Professor Tim Guilford, with whom you should be familiar from the pages of the book, and others, established a fund at the University of Oxford called Save our Shearwaters (SOS) to do exactly this.

This is how he describes his work on behalf of the Balearic shearwater:

Europe's rarest seabird is the Balearic shearwater (*Puffinus mauretanicus*), which breeds in the Mediterranean and migrates north into the Atlantic in the summer. It is seen increasingly off Britain with perhaps a quarter of the world population visibly using our seas at times in late summer. But it is critically endangered, and faces as a species a deeply uncertain future because of threats from fisheries bycatch and climate change at sea, and predation pressure and human disturbance at the breeding colonies. Despite this, still remarkably little is known about its behaviour and ecological needs: knowledge which must underpin conservation efforts to avert its extinction.

At Oxford our team is collaborating with Spanish, French and UK conservation scientists to try to fill important knowledge gaps and raise awareness of the species' plight. Using state-of-the-art miniature tracking technologies, we are tackling fundamental questions about where and how breeding birds feed (and how this relates to human fisheries), where they oversummer, and their patterns of colony use in the pre-breeding months. We are now trying to determine the provenance of birds using UK waters, which we think may be non- or pre-breeders becoming increasingly dependent on our waters as the changing climate drives important marine resources north. And we are setting up longer term monitoring efforts to help assess key changes in breeding success, overwinter survival, and the patterns of breeding and migration.

If you would like to support in any way, please check it all out by following the link below.

https://www.development.ox.ac.uk/
save-our-shearwaters

Very many thanks.

BIBLIOGRAPHY

Strictly speaking, this is just a list of books that I read, or re-read, in the writing of my own. Apart from the first two, which I drew on heavily, the other books helped provide for me the connecting nature, science and sometimes philosophy that became the mortar around the bricks of the shearwater's story. No man, as John Donne pointed out, is an island entire of itself, just as no bird's story can be told without reference to the wider context of the world it lives in, and the creatures it co-exists with. Taken together, this list has given me a deep appreciation of the seabird's beautiful world, as well as its fragility.

The Manx Shearwater, Dr Michael Brooke (T & A.D. Poyser, 1990)

Shearwaters, R.M. Lockley (J.M. Dent & Sons, 1942)

Far From Land, Dr Michael Brooke (Princeton University Press, 2018)

Ocean Birds, Lars Löfgren (Knopf, 1984)

British Birds, F.B. Kirkman and F.C.R. Jourdain (Nelson, 1930)

Birds Britannica, Mark Cocker (Random House, 2020)

Dream Island, R.M. Lockley (Little Toller Books, 2016)

Letters from Skokholm, R.M. Lockley (J.M. Dent & Sons, 1947)

Ocean Wanderers, R.M. Lockley (David & Charles, 1974)

Skomer Island Nature Reserve, Annual Report and Census (2018)

Albatrosses, Petrels and Shearwaters of the World, Derek Onley and Paul Scofield (Helm, 2007)

The Seabird's Cry, Adam Nicolson (William Collins, 2017)

Petrels Night and Day, Magnus Robb (The Sound Approach, 2008)

Curlew Moon, Mary Colwell (William Collins, 2018)

Time to Fly: Exploring Bird Migration, Jim Flegg (BTO, 2004)

The Birds of the Western Palearctic, David W. Snow and Christopher Perrins (Oxford University Press, 1997)

The Seafarers, Stephen Rutt (Elliott & Thompson, 2019)

Our Place, Mark Cocker (Jonathan Cape, 2018)

'Navigation in the Manx Shearwater', G. Matthews (PhD diss., University of Cambridge, 1953)

A Conspiracy of Ravens, Bill Oddie (Bodleian Library, 2012)

Bird Sense, Tim Birkhead (Bloomsbury, 2012)

A Short Philosophy of Birds, Philippe Dubois and Elise Rousseau (W.H. Allen, 2019)

The Genius of Birds, Jennifer Ackerman (Corsair, 2016)

There is No Planet B, Mike Berners-Lee (Cambridge University Press, 2019)

The Wonderful Mr Willughby: The First True Ornithologist, Tim Birkhead (Bloomsbury, 2018)

Oceans of Birds, Tony Soper (David & Charles, 1989)

Birds of the Atlantic Ocean, Ted Stokes (Country Life Books, 1968)

To the Ends of the Earth: Ireland's place in Bird Migration, Anthony McGeehan (The Collins Press, 2018)

The Running Sky, Tim Dee (Jonathan Cape, 2009)

The Sea Inside, Philip Hoare (Fourth Estate, 2013)

The Herring Gull's World, Niko Tinbergen (Harper Torchbooks, 1960)

The Snow Geese, William Fiennes (Picador, 2002)

The Idea of North, Peter Davidson (Reaktion Books, 2005)

Islands Beyond the Horizon, Roger Lovegrove (OUP, 2012)

Adventures Among Birds, W.H. Hudson (J.M. Dent & Sons, 1923)

Sightlines, Kathleen Jamie (Sort of Books, 2012)

Love of Country, Madeleine Bunting (Granta, 2016)

Farmageddon, Philip Lymbery with Isabel Oakeshott (Bloomsbury, 2015)

Night Falls on Ardnamurchan, Alasdair Maclean (Penguin, 1984)

Wilfrid Freeman, The Genius Behind Allied Survival and Air Supremacy, 1939–45, Anthony Furse (The History Press, 2000)

The Summer Isles, Philip Marsden (Granta, 2019)

The Isle of Muck: a Short Guide, Lawrence MacEwen

Aves de Sudamerica – Guia de Campo Collins, Jorge Rodríguez Mata and Francisco Erize (Letemendia, 2006)

Others

DEFRA reports: http://jncc.defra.gov.uk/page-3120

http://www.birdlife.org/action/campaigns/save_the_albatross/fao_doc3.pdf

'Breeding Biology of Manx Shearwater', Michael Brooke (PhD diss., University of Oxford, 1977)

ACKNOWLEDGEMENTS

Many people have helped me on my year-long journey, from wardens to volunteers, boatmen to folklore experts, students to providers of beds and cups of tea, and I am hugely grateful to them all. Conservation work of any sort, I have found out, brings you together with some of the biggest-hearted people on the planet. However, one group has gone above and beyond the call of duty. I have been constantly amazed by the generosity of the bird science community, who have allowed me their precious time and also free access to their painstaking research. This includes work not yet peer-reviewed or published, on the basis that they felt it gave me a more complete picture, and that they trusted me not to quote it in the text before formal publication. I am acutely aware that much of this story draws deeply on research that other people have worked on for years, and I only hope that the book itself does it, and their efforts, justice. If I single out two, it would be Mike Brooke, for taking my first approach so seriously and pointing me in all the right directions, and Tim Guilford for becoming my unofficial tutor, co-worker at a new charity, and friend. They are truly the godfathers to the current generation of Manx shearwaters. The list below is sadly not exhaustive, but my gratitude extends to the very many people who helped me out.

I am also truly grateful to both my agent, Clare Grist Taylor, and my publisher and editor, Duncan Heath of Icon Books, for believing in and supporting this project from the very start, and for tolerating the slings and arrows of delay that anyone trying to do just about anything in early 2020 had to face. Plus all at Icon, especially Andrew Furlow, Ruth Killick, Hanna Milner and Hamza Jahanzeb.

Finally, my wife Caroline, who painted the beautiful front cover of the book, and tolerated my long absences, both physical and mental, while I was writing it. This is obviously for you, too, and with very much love.

Oxford University
Professor Tim Guilford
Professor Chris Perrins
Joe Wynn
Dr Ollie Padget
Natasha Gillies
Sophie Wilcox (Radcliffe Science Library)

Cambridge University
Dr Michael Brooke

Sheffield University
Professor Tim Birkhead

Cork, Republic of Ireland
Professor John Quinn
Sam Bayley
Tom Kelly
Steve Wing
Jeremy and Julia Gould

Skomer
Nathan Wilkie
Sylwia Zbijewska